ON GROWING OLDER

* Eugene C. Bianchi

ON GROWING OLDER

A Personal Guide to Life after Thirty-five

illustrations by Lee Lawson

CROSSROAD · NEW YORK

1986
The Crossroad Publishing Company
370 Lexington Avenue, New York, N.Y. 10017

Library of Congress Cataloging in Publication Data

Bianchi, Eugene C.
On growing older.
1. Middle age – Religious life.   I. Title.
BV4579.5.B53   1985   248.8'4   85–11346
ISBN 0-8245-0700-2

CONTENTS

INTRODUCTION

This book of reflections aims at deepening our experience of our own aging process. The key word is "experience." Each meditation gives us food for thought, but the main purpose of these mental reflections is to shape a context for experiencing through meditation our personal attitudes and feelings about aging.

Recently a middle-aged friend told me about a deeply moving experience with his twelve-year-old son. My friend had taken his octogenarian father into his home for the last year of the old man's life. The father was cared for materially and spiritually in a community of loved ones. This in itself is a rare occurrence today. The children participated in various aspects of the grandfather's final season. At the burial, the boy turned toward his father and said: "Now I know what to do. When you are old, dad, I will take care of you, and when you die, I will bury you." Neither father or son will forget the dramatic and demanding experience of that last year of the grandfather's life, his death, and those direct, simple words of graveside commitment.

Meditations on aging cannot replicate the profound event experienced by that family, which lived day and night with the dying elder. But the meditations attempt to lead us in a vicarious way toward inner experience that involves the whole person. A few minutes spent in the guided-imagery exercises transforms us into actors on the stage of our imagination. We recognize feelings repressed or neglected. On the stage of contemplation we can anticipate problematic events and rehearse our responses to them. Like an unexpected gift, a new insight may descend on us in meditation. So many things today militate against creative aging and dignified dying that we need to take some time out for this theater of the soul.

Meditation on aging as presented here seeks to help us fix our attention on evocative words and images. Such contemplation is a process of centering our consciousness, of focusing on important personal issues associated with aging. By repeating this inward process, we gradually discover our own deeper resources. In meditation, we open the door of our soul from the inside, allowing a more dynamic interchange of world and self.

Most of us move through our days and years as though we were set on automatic pilot. We have learned certain routine patterns of coping with life at home or in the workplace. By slowing down the hectic pace of the mind, meditation permits us to center our consciousness on important problems that confront us in midlife and elderhood. Instead of concealing human dilemmas that only increase with age, the contemplative focus teaches us to dwell upon issues, feel their intensity as much as possible, and move through them toward a more enlightened way of being in the world. This stop-look-listen activity of the mind and heart leads to a gradual change of consciousness. We come to see more things as they really are, rather than as we have disguised them. Whether the topic be detachment, loneliness, love, or hope, meditating can crack open our rigid ego defenses, broaden our perspective, and make us more porous to the reality and the promise of our personal history. The insights of authentic meditation may not give us immediate peace; our fears and worries may even intensify for a time. But as we let ourselves experience these anxieties in meditation, we break through to deeper levels of our soul where the problems can be both sustained and transformed. In this way, meditation becomes a way of personal and transpersonal growth. Not only is our own inner balance restored, but we are better able to redirect our energy outwardly.

Midlife is a particularly good season for appreciating this paradox about meditation: The cultivation of inwardness frees us to relate more creatively with others. Inner deepening and outward growth are strongly complementary, not contradictory. Meditation teaches us to be solitaries who embrace the world in a more altruistic way. We come to understand how our aging experiences link us with others in suffering, loving, working, and seeking greater meaning. These meditations, therefore, have an ethical thrust, an orientation toward a more peaceful, just, and caring world. Such a moral dimension is not imposed on the contemplative, as one might place a coat or a blanket over him or her. Rather, ethical sensitivity and compassion arise naturally from those deeper chambers of the soul where we encounter our common humanity and our mutual responsibility. The ideal of the peacemaking elder sums up the age-old theme of the contemplative in action. The final, "outward" aspect of meditation is also oddly inward, in that it becomes an approach to the divine source of existence within ourselves. As we learn to listen to inner voices, we discern the pain and the peace of sharing in the mystery that embraces us all. This transpersonal experience within and without opens us to a knowledge of the heart, to a new way of being religious in the world as aging persons.

To realize such excellent goals of meditation, certain disciplined steps are important. There is no one set of techniques that can dispose us toward the deeper experiences of meditation. But contemplative masters, East and West, point out helpful disciplines that can be adapted to one's particular circumstances. Let us discuss here the few guidelines that pertain to each of the twenty-four exercises in this book. These aids to contemplation relate mainly to the second part of each chapter; the first part of each aims at placing the mind in a reflective context on a particular topic. The real work of contemplating and personalizing these themes occurs in the guided-imagery sections at the end of each chapter.

The following is a short outline of useful points for meditating:

1. *Silence and Solitude.* Of course, we can meditate in just about any place. But it is generally easier, especially at the start, to seek out a quiet and solitary environment. A relatively small group of people can also meditate together in silence and then share insights and images. Silence allows us to concentrate on inner voices and feelings. It detaches us from the usual distractions by which we keep our inner self at bay.

2. *Time and Place.* This is a matter of preference and common sense. Some will find early morning to be the best time; others will choose another period in keeping with their responsibilities and temperament. Any amount of meditation time is good, but at least ten to twenty minutes allow us to dwell on images and

scenarios so that they reveal themselves with greater influence. Choose a special, congenial space and time that is set aside for meditation. The point here is to associate a given place with the contemplative function. Such a spot takes on an aura of consecrated ground, away from desks and tables where so many other activities happen. Such a place can facilitate entrance into a contemplative mood. Again, many other places will be suitable for meditation, but the special space becomes the usual gateway to the inner journey. Another type of inward space for meditation can be cleared and developed. Through guided imagery we can locate ourselves in a forest clearing or on a mountain or by the sea; various guests can imaginatively enter that space.

3. *Posture.* The general rule would be to have our bodies in a comfortable but centered position; the main point of bodily posture is to reduce distractions. Some will find an accommodated form of the lotus posture very helpful; this position seems to center the body in a way that stimulates mental focus. A comfortable, seated position is fine. But here it is advisable to place both feet on the floor or ground, sit in a firm seat with one's back straight and unsupported. Hands can rest quietly on one's thighs, possibly with palms turned upward in a gesture of receptivity. It usually helps to close one's eyes when moving inward. Some may find a standing but stationary position congenial. With enough experience we can learn to transfer meditative techniques to less strenuous modes of walking. The main idea is to select postures that foster rather than hinder inwardness.

4. *Breathing.* In this matter especially, we can learn a good deal from Eastern techniques and purposes. Each of the following meditations will call for a brief set of breathing exercises in the beginning of the process. For our purposes, it will be sufficient to slowly draw in a deep breath, hold it for a few seconds, and slowly release it. Doing this a dozen times has a calming effect. It also seems to aid in clearing the mind for awhile of cluttering thoughts; moreover, the deep breathing can further awaken us by promoting a better oxygen supply. As we do the initial breathing, we focus on the process itself of inhaling and exhaling. Such concentration pulls us away from distractions and fosters a sense of physical rhythms in unity with our natural environment. Again, concentration on breathing becomes a

centering activity. Many aspects of guided imagery can be associated with the fundamental action of breathing. Mental distractions will quite naturally pull us this way and that at any stage of meditation. This should not be a cause for discouragement; rather, we must simply accept the ever fluid state of mind, gently drawing it back to the subject of meditation. Focused breathing promotes fixed attention to a word, a concept, an object, an image, a sound, or even to a bodily function.

5. *Text and Journal.* This book may be used in a number of ways. Some may discover useful thoughts by merely reading through it. Others may wish to explore in a more intentionally meditative style themes of particular value to them at a certain stage of life. Still others could choose to make the text a means by which they learn to improve their meditative ability while, at the same time, focusing on important issues of midlife and elderhood. The book could become a starting point for small self-help groups who wish to expand these themes in discussion after an initial period of meditation. The volume may also be of service in retreat situations focusing on issues of maturity. The meditations would fit in well with personal journal-keeping. The latter is an extremely valuable practice for persons in their middle and later years. The personal journal, unlike a diary or a memoir, calls for deeper reflection on feelings and thoughts arising from problematic or conflicting areas of life. Meditation and journal-writing reciprocally stimulate each other.

6. *Mantra.* The mantra is a short phrase or a word-coupling that evokes a special energy and purpose for its users. In American Indian history, youths sought to receive their own song in the Vision Quest. Eastern seekers of deeper meaning and experience formulated or were given special mantras that served a number of integrating goals. The use of mantra-like phrases has its own tradition in Western spirituality. Examples of mantras from traditional sources might be: *Om mani padme hum*, "the jewel in the lotus of the heart" (Buddhist), or *Barukh attah Adonai*, "Blessed art thou, O Lord" (Jewish), or "Lord Jesus Christ" (Eastern Christianity). Yet any number of suitable contemporary phrases would be appropriate, such as "Peace and Unity," "Loving-Kindness," "Oneness Respecting Differences." The repetition of a mantra during parts of a meditation acts like

an integrating and expanding song of this particular individual. By the quiet utterance of mantras that summarize our special callings and our deeper personalities, we summon up healing and illuminating energies. One may use traditional phrases or invent others particularly suited to one's spiritual-humanistic orientations. In trying situations, repetition of a mantra can bring peace and perspective to our spirits. Some individuals have also mastered techniques of self-hypnosis that can be employed in furthering meditative concentration.

7. *Drawings*. Lee Lawson's evocative line drawings are meant not only to beautify the book but also to serve as a form of contemporary mandala. In many cultures, mandalas in carvings, architecture, and in graphic art portrayed a dynamic unity of opposites. They helped the meditating person to concentrate on a unified complexity while he or she sought to integrate disparate aspects of life. Lawson's contemplative outlook speaks for itself in these drawings, as they open up to multiple symbols for reflecting on the aging process.

I am deeply indebted to a number of persons who helped me produce this book. Lee Lawson, an artist and friend, contributed the drawings from her outstanding collection of paintings and other artworks. Ali Crown coaxed the computer to remember and pour forth various versions of the manuscript. Henry Carrigan, Susie Sherrill, and my wife, Victoria, edited the work and made many helpful suggestions for improving it. Connie Brillhart removed various hurdles on the road toward publication. To these and to others in the Emory University community, I extend sincere gratitude.

In a wider sense of gratitude, this book is dedicated to all those elders who, by word and example, helped us embrace and share life. Some of these older ones have faces and voices for us. Others enter our stories in more remote but telling ways. To all of these teachers of creative aging we offer thanks.

CONTENDING WITH AGEISM

Aging is a quiet problem. As children we notice older people: a grandparent leaning on a cane or an aunt with joints swollen with arthritis. Parents may have told us that the dog is very old; we accept this knowledge, but without relating it to ourselves. Moreover, getting old happens so slowly: to the child's gaze, parents and other elders seem fixed in their respective ages. Yet we subtly learn to think about being old as a negative condition. It shows itself in wrinkles, slowing down, reminiscing, illness, and death. It stands over against health, vitality, and beauty.

This vision of aging is nothing new; children of all times have observed these diminishments. The special dimension today is the context in which aging occurs. We live in a highly technological environment that honors youth and mobility. We are geared to speed and productivity: producing goods and services in volume as quickly as possible for the highest monetary yield. Society rewards such activity and associates it with relative youthfulness. The old (and in many cases the middle aged) become obstacles to our culture's most prized values. As long as old items fit into the technological order, they assume a certain value. For example, people place a premium on old furniture as an antique; it is scarce and in demand for beauty as well as function. Antique cars can enjoy a similar fate. As we move toward living things, the scale of values changes. An ancient tree may be admired in a protected park, but its destiny falls into jeopardy when viewed through the commercial eyes of real-estate developers. Ultimately, the yardstick of life or death becomes utility and profit.

Such is the context of contemporary ageism, an attitude that discriminates against the old simply because they are no longer young. Ageism, just like old age, has a long history. Literary and historical records reveal sentiments that deprecate elders for alleged moral, mental, and physical deficiencies. We didn't invent ageism in the twentieth century, but we did maximize its devastating stereotypes in the technological age. We have always feared death, which stalks us especially in the guise of the elderly. Demeaning humor about old age expresses a defense mechanism against our own fear of personal decline and death. It will happen to thee and to thee but not to me. Such is the futile delusion of the ageist mentality, which in the end destroys its own future. The technological era has elevated ageism from an aberrant fear to a universal creed.

Ageist stereotypes seep steadily into our conscious and unconscious minds. Media images often present old age as a period of moral, mental, and physical decrepitude. We are told that the elderly are too senile to exercise morally responsible choices. So much has been said about Altzheimer's disease in recent years that an image of universal mental collapse attaches itself to the aging process. It is profitable for pharmaceutical companies to present the old as major consumers of tonics, medications, and drugs. The resultant image of the elderly bespeaks weakness, sickness, immobility, dependence, and sexlessness.

The saddest aspect of ageist stereotypes is that, by gradually incorporating them into our thinking, they become self-fulfilling prophecies. We imitate in our lives these destructive cultural images of aging. We act out what we imagine. The middle-aged as well as the old fall victim to this process. Men in their forties overcompensate for their fear of aging by competing physically and professionally with younger men on the latter's terms.

Women in midlife succumb to every fad for dieting and for cosmetic rejuvenation. The old stumble meekly to the sidelines of life, convinced by self-embraced stereotypes that the game is to the young. This pattern of our society nullifies skills, experience, and wisdom of age to the detriment of all.

How do we break the shackles of ageist stereotypes in our lives? We must first encounter and make peace with our finite life span. This is not the task of one meditation, or of one year of contemplation; rather it is a lifetime development of one's own spirituality as a limited creature of nature with splendid potentials. Ageist stereotypes ultimately build on the common ground of the fearful denial of personal decline and death. We deride what we fear, as if derision could stave it off.

But the conquest of stereotypes must be taken in stages. The peaceful acceptance of our own mortality constitutes an advanced phase of psychospiritual development. We must first explore our stereotypes about aging.

Begin your meditation with a few minutes of deep breathing exercises to center and relax yourself. Close your eyes, sit in a comfortable but erect posture. Focus on your breathing process; you are drawing in life-sustaining air and you are releasing tensions with each relaxing exhalation. Imagine yourself as an older man or woman. Try to visualize your appearance at sixty-five or seventy-five; perhaps looking at a family album will help the process. You will most likely look something like those elder parents or relatives. Notice how younger people will see you in an ageist environment. On a physical level, they will imagine you sickly and weak, in need of special protection and care. Oppose these thoughts by dwelling pictorially in imagination on a vital, strong, and self-determining image of yourself. In your mind's eye, spend some time watching the elderly you moving about. Are you stooped or erect? See yourself meeting and dealing with persons of all ages. Portray yourself walking briskly, engaging in pleasureable activities. You reject the stereotypes of age and decline, letting them flow away like water off a rock.

Your demeanor in modest but in telling ways also shatters the physical images of ageism.

What about your mental abilities? Think of some areas of life about which you wish to learn more. See yourself studying these areas. Maybe this will take place in a school milieu or perhaps through private pursuits. By reading, reflecting, and discussing, you can keep your memory intact. You can also integrate the knowledge and experience that a long life has accumulated. See yourself with the intellectual curiosity of an elderly Margaret Mead, an Alfred Whitehead, or a Thomas Edison. Imagine an elderly you that is a model of appreciative and critical thinking, gaining the esteem and encouragement of younger people. You will shatter the stereotypes of mental collapse for yourself and for them.

From whatever field you know best, choose a model of moral responsibility and decision-making. Perhaps you will visualize someone in the arts like Picasso, vitally creative into nine decades. Or perhaps you will focus on an elder statesman like Averill Harriman, negotiating disputes among diplomats. Perhaps the image of Dorothy Day serving the homeless and furthering the cause of nonviolence will form on your imaginary screen. Picture the elder you – as depicted in that album photo – involved in and committed to some universal values and needs of humanity. In your own circle of associates, determine now to repulse the stereotypes of irresponsible elderhood. As the paradigms of ageism become less true for you, they will also fade for those young persons influenced by you.

In and through this physical, mental, and moral imagining, you are opening yourself to the spiritual dimensions of aging. You will also see yourself as an elder sharing the depth of a rich wisdom that has developed from leaving a window of consciousness open to the eternal. Through prayer and meditation, you have been willing to face life's risks and the final unknown of death. Your spirituality will uplift those around you as they contemplate their own aging.

·2

LETTING-GO

A central insight of Buddhism shapes the core of healthy and creative aging: Stop clinging to things and unreal expectations in life if you wish to find happiness and inner peace. It is with some hesitation that I translate the message of the Four Noble Truths into the Western language of happiness and peace. To make these terms more accurate in the Buddhist vision, we have to purify them of bland notions concerning comfort and seeming security. Rather, happiness and peace are deeper states of soul consonant with hardship, discipline, questing, and commitment. But back to the main point: the cessation of selfish craving and clinging to material things or to ideologies. We can further translate this insight into an attitude of letting-go. The Christian or Jewish idiom would call it the spirit of detachment that disposes one to live by faith.

Why is detachment of letting-go crucial for the process of creative aging? To answer this query, we need to review some basics concerning the human life span. For survival's sake, childhood is necessarily a time of craving satisfactions for the self. For the most part, children focus mainly on their personal wants and needs; and what's more, this is fine. They need support and

·5

security from their parents and others. But notice also a funda-mental human pattern, begun in childhood, and easily main-tained through succeeding stages of life. Like children, we con-tinue to crave things, praise, and power as if these supports could stave off forever our decline and death. The pattern of clinging, craving, and gathering to oneself becomes a destruc-tive style in the phases of middle age and elderhood. This un-transformed pattern of childhood gives us false security. It also is at the root of many social evils.

Midlife offers a most appropriate time for altering the attach-ment rhythms of childhood and youth. In middle age we can know our finitude in a personal and gripping way. Time is not on our side. We are mortal and no clinging or craving will make us immortal, will preserve us against our own death and dying process. Moreover, by midlife—if we haven't been mired totally in our childish death-denying culture—we are ready for serious transformations or conversions of heart. Perhaps for the first time in our lives we stand prepared to let go. Much depends on these transitions from craving to caring, from getting to shar-ing, from attachment to detachment. The deepening of one's own humanity and spirituality flows from such transformation. Moreover, the possibility of a new social ethic, based on a spirit of stewardship for all life, requires such conversions among a sizeable portion of the nation.

Authentic letting-go, however, results from a subtle cadence of detachment and attachment. We are not merely to cast off the illusory securities of earlier days, as if such throwing over-board of dangerous cargo could of itself guide us on the journey. Just as nature abhors a vacuum, so does our soul. The ideal is not to drift endlessly in the sea of life, subject to prevailing winds. Rather, the jettisoning of useless baggage allows us to vector more swiftly in new directions. In the contemplative mo-ment of letting-go we may find ourselves becalmed for awhile. But when the spirit blows again, we must be willing to risk new attachments. The important point concerns the nature of these new attachments. Are they still the impossible, anxiety-produc-ing cravings of childhood for immortality and total security? Or does a spirit of greater empathy and universal care pervade the new attachments?

Begun in midlife especially, the cycles of letting-go with their rhythms of critique and detachment are joined to new attachments, which are themselves always subject to review and transformation. This alchemy within us can lead to an elderhood of spiritual advancement and ever greater service to the human community. The Buddhist understanding of these truths has affinities with the Christian spirit of the Beatitudes. The Buddha emphasized the impermanence and interrelatedness of all reality, calling for experiences of detachment in order to open our eyes (to become enlightened) to the way things really are. Jesus in the Beatitudes blesses the attitude of those who let go the false securities of dominant power, worldly wealth, and ego inflation. Yet detachment from illusion becomes the catalyst for more valuable attachments such as peacemaking and personal integrity: "Blessed are the poor in spirit," "Blessed are the peacemakers," "Blessed are the pure in heart." This embracing of deeper values constitutes a high ideal for elderhood.

Much of what we were taught in youth to crave as sources of security has only made us less secure as adults. Perhaps we were told that money would preserve us, influential friends would protect us, positions of power would keep us from diminishment. Close your eyes and draw into your imaginary vision the faces and voices of those who gave you the secrets of security. If the messages were about material things, try to recall what some of these were. When you have located the early cravings for various possessions, draw a deep breath, holding it, allowing the indrawn air to loosen the particular attachment from its long hold over you. Then exhale while picturing this desire being washed out of your being. Repeat the exercise for as many times as seems comfortable. Return to it at a different time, because the deeply ingrained desires on which you built a life will not be changed without discipline or dedication. Do not interpret this releasing of material possessions as a disparagement of things or of nature. Rather it is a false, harmful understanding of the place of material things in your life that you are gradually expelling.

We necessarily attach ourselves by emotional ties to parents long before we consciously reflect on these relationships. These primal ties are vitally important for shaping a secure sense of self, for forming our ability to love and to trust. But there is another aspect of family attachment that subconsciously teaches us to attach ourselves to influential others who are expected to carry on the parental function of protecting and preserving us throughout life. We transfer this dependence onto spouses, mentors, friends, and other persons seen as sources of power and security. It is rare wisdom to understand that we are ultimately alone before the great challenges of life. This is not at all an argument against the joys and benefits of community and friendship that can support us in valuable ways. But we will never grow to our full stature in the aging process until we are willing to journey alone inwardly into our unconscious well-springs and journey alone outwardly toward the existential limits of our mortal place in nature. Reflect on parents and relatives, and move to teachers, associates, and directors, possibly even political or religious figures. Enter into the breathing exercise with the important individual mirrored in your imagination. Be grateful for whatever blessing that person has conferred on you. But as you draw in breath, let it gently lift each of these individuals and release them from you, because you need to meet certain challenges alone. You will never be free until you can be at peace in your own primordial aloneness.

We scheme and strive for honor and power. We place our self-worth on the acclaim of others or on the dominance we are able to exercise over persons and events. Of course, honor and power are not the only motivations for our action, nor is there anything wrong with enjoying praise from others for the exercise of our energies to make something happen. This meditation is not a condemnation of honor and power. Rather, it is an attempt to loosen our attachments to these motivators as fundamental to our sense of worthiness. Recall the honors that may have come to you in life or the honors for which you especially long. Draw them onto your imaginative stream one by one as you inhale and hold your breath. As you release your breath, say explicitly to yourself that your dignity and peace of soul do not depend on this or that honor. Do the same exercise with your attachments to forms of dominant power, whether you employ it toward your children, your spouse, or toward colleagues and associates. Dominative power is the opposite of enabling power. The former makes us feel important and enduring because we seem to be in control of persons or institutions. Enabling power aims at helping others to develop according to their full potentials. Formulate imaginatively those situations in which you indulge in the attachment to dominative power. Release with your breathing these dimensions of yourself.

As we detach ourselves from clinging to false securities, we must also risk new, flexible, and reformable attachments. An ideal aspect of midlife and elderhood consists in pursuing deeper and broader values. This means a richer attachment to dialogue with the resources of one's own soul, to the cultivation of friendships, and to involvement in universal concerns for human rights, justice, and peace. In the breathing exercise, focus on some of these attachments as they might pertain to you. As you inhale, pull the life-giving oxygen around this image in your mind to give it sustenance, helping it to take root in you as you grow toward an elderhood of generosity and commitment.

·3·

SUFFERING DIMINISHMENT

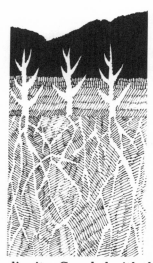 I have asked people to write down their personal fears about old age. Almost invariably they list the prospect of mental and physical decline with its various forms of suffering. The bodily and psychological dimensions of this are closely intertwined. Physical illness is not only associated with pain and weakness, but also with loss of control over one's own destiny. Hardening of the arteries raises the specter of memory loss and of social alienation. They fear a prolonged decline that may involve the use of sophisticated medical technology to keep them alive at a very questionable level of quality and dignity. Coupled with these fears is that of becoming a financial and familial burden to others. Thus the suffering connected with older age is complex: physical, mental, and social. All these factors blend into a picture of a frail, confused, isolated, and socially outcast existence. Since this vision of old age consciously or unconsciously invades our outlook, we avoid reflection on our elderhood. The vague but terrifying shadow of suffering and diminishment keeps us from fruitful meditation. Let us look more steadfastly at this reality that will affect many of us in different ways.

We might start by mitigating somewhat our fears of this

decline. We have all experienced pain and suffering in our lives to this point; we have developed certain coping mechanisms for this natural condition of existence. Most of us have weathered physical injury and sickness to enjoy good health again. Although our resiliency will be somewhat lessened with age, we should be able to make it successfully through many of the sufferings that await us. Moreover, the all-too-universal image of diminishment painted above is cast erroneously over the whole span of elderhood. This is particularly unfortunate because it hinders people from thinking creatively about their own aging. Yet a great number of persons live into an eighth and even ninth decade with good health of mind and body. Although these positive considerations are true and necessary to balance the dire stereotype about old age, the last phase of our lives will most likely bring special forms of suffering and diminishment. By facing this reality in earlier periods of life, we can both tame some of its terror and also derive positive aspects for our development. Teilhard de Chardin summed up this focus in his phrase "growth through diminishment."

Teilhard was certainly not embracing pain and disability for themselves in a masochistic way. Rather he understood through his own experiences—from his time in the trenches of the First World War through a long career as a visionary paleontologist—that adversity could become the crucible for refining the human spirit. Suffering and diminishment have a way of breaking through the façade of our self-deception. At the heart of the deception we work on ourselves is the tenacious belief that it (whatever hardship) won't happen to me. So intense is our fear of serious problems that we delude ourselves into believing that it (all manner of good things) will happen to us. Of course, there is a place for desiring achievements and blessings; but it can become an infantile illusion, blocking growth of personality, to expect a perfectly harmonious world for the self. Suffering shocks us, disturbing the veil of deception. It forces us to reassess the truth about life, about our lives. Our minds are both enlightened and humbled before the fragility and the contingency of existence. We may, perhaps for the first time, come to see the world as it truly is; only then can we evaluate honestly our commitments toward creation. Suffering reminds us of our finitude, of our deeper fellowship with all creatures in this limited world.

Some persons are able to build monuments from adversity. A mother lost her only child in a tragic accident; over the course of many years she acted as a benevolent and inspiring foster mother to many other children. Her personal diminishment as a mother was turned into a monument of caring for many young lives. As we meet the sufferings, mental and physical, that aging brings us, we are invited to learn greater compassion for others. The word "compassion" derives from Latin, meaning to "suffer with," that is, to feel empathy with the pain of fellow creatures. True compassion, not mere sentimental sympathy, moves us beyond knowledge about our common lot to the deeper reaches of personal becoming. For the compassion experienced through our own diminishments motivates us to ethical action. Albert Schweitzer exemplified a famous elder who despite, or perhaps because of, hardships in later life, provided a caring environment for the sick in Africa. Albert Einstein, as an old man, moved to ever larger human concerns about peace in the world, trying to awaken the intellectual community and the nations at large to the need for action to prevent the calamity of modern war. It is the development of such a spirit that Teilhard envisioned in the evolution of mind on our planet; growth through diminishment reveals a final flowering of the life span. As we enter a downward slope on the physical level, we have the opportunity through our heightened compassion to bring about a spiritual ascent with great social benefits.

Growth through diminishment marks the difference between a creative elderhood and one increasingly narrowed into sadness, isolation, and even bitterness. Yet it is vital in youth or midlife to begin rehearsing the dialogue with our particular sufferings and diminishments, especially those that we are not able to overcome. Without such earlier training, it is unlikely that we will cope well with the more grievous problems of elderhood. By meditating on this topic in our middle years, we can become more truthful persons. Truthfulness means letting our existence as it really is enter consciousness without the illusions that blind us from living honestly. This truthfulness allows us to speak and act more courageously, because we grasp our condition as suffering survivors who have very little to lose by honesty. Reflection on growth through diminishment also helps us lessen egotism, while opening the way for greater self-esteem. The egotist resides ultimately in illusory clouds of his or her own making; the egotist refuses to learn the truth about human existence: that we are mutually interdependent fellow sufferers on planet earth. The egotist cannot face death, the ultimate diminishment. As we deal truthfully with our smaller "deaths," however, self-esteem grows. For we come to realize that our worth does not depend on the say-so of our betters or on the acclaim of institutions. Self-esteem is based rather on our acceptance of ourselves as wonderous creatures who can live creatively with the pain of life.

Place yourself in a comfortable spot where you feel particularly at ease. As you begin to do slow breathing exercises with eyes closed, draw these two pictures into your imagination. One is that of a child holding a finger to her one open eye. She is blotting out a wider vision by concentrating all her attention on the finger. The second frame portrays an older man sitting on his porch, looking out into the yard through ten square feet of screening.

These images set the theme for our reflection on suffering and diminishment. We are too often like the child rather than like the old man. We focus so intensely on our disabilities that we exclude from sight other vistas of opportunity. The old man may not be as mobile or as healthy as he once was, but from his limited window on the world, he observes and shares in a great deal of life through the ten square feet of vision. He can enjoy the beauty of nature, the changing rituals of its creatures, and he can look out toward new horizons.

Before the old man could view the world in a creative way, he had to learn to make peace with his limitations. Let us attempt a few exercises for such management of suffering. First, recognize and be thankful for your dependable bodily functions such as sight and hearing. Lift into your imaginative vision some part of your body or some overall condition that represents physical deficiency. Speak inwardly to that part of you which is a source of suffering and worry. The dialogue might go like this: I am sensing this organ or process in my own body; I am approaching it in a friendly way, accepting this part of me that hurts or fails to operate as it should. As I embrace this weaker aspect of my being, I am showing compassion for myself, making friends with my shortcomings. I am not rejecting these dimensions of myself as enemies. Because I choose to love my body even as afflicted, I am able to release healing energies for its betterment, and I can also unshackle my mind from further anxiety about my condition. From making peace with my diminishments, I free myself from their domination over me; I am liberated to open up to others and their concerns. Many of us suffer more than we need to because we do not communicate with our own bodies. Reflect with gratitude on how well this body has served me as I have aged over many years.

I am getting older. My body reminds me of this happening through certain sufferings and diminishments. Yet all this, too, is for my growth in wisdom and love. I realize that whatever physical or mental injuries come to me, I as this unique person am not identified with them. I am not my body nor am I this less well portion of it. I am not the individual defined by this or that social role, by holding such and such an office or by being seen as a retired, senior citizen. What I truly am is not identified by my more or less well body or by social role or status. I am this special person, this continuously remembered being who is not one with sufferings or diminishments. If I am in contact with the insights from my unconscious, I understand all the more that I am not my body, my ideas alone, or my public identities. This meditative exercise serves as a useful complement to that of understanding my connection with my body. While I need to cultivate a friendly attitude toward the physical me, I must also learn not to identify my person fully with my body or my social classification.

This rhythm of solidarity and separation permits me to grow toward elderhood as a free human being. As I learn from physical and psychological challenges to discover my true self, I become open to others, to nature, and to God in a deeper way. I realize through my sufferings that I am one with other humans across all national and racial demarcations. Their pain is my pain; this summons up my caring commitment to alleviate the destructive dimensions of our mutual injuries. In the family of pain, suffering, and diminishment, we are all brothers and sisters who need one another. The natural world teaches me constantly both resignation and resiliency in the face of decline. Look at the trees; see how they have an alloted time before they fall to make space for new life. Yet notice also how they adapt to and incorporate various injuries as they grow stronger and higher. As I find my more authentic self by dealing creatively with suffering and diminishment, I age in God. I and the world are enveloped in a God who experiences the suffering and diminishment of the world. My passage through the pain of life becomes in faith redemptive as I share in the redemptive suffering and becoming of God.

As you finish your meditation on suffering and diminishment, let the main insights for you linger on and be nurtured by your quiet, rhythmic breathing.

·4

DEALING WITH LONELINESS

Learning to deal wisely with one's lone-liness is essential for creative aging. For in the normal process of middle age and elderhood, we experience in acute and painful ways our separation from individuals, even those closest to us. As we recognize these persons as truly other, we sense a certain standing apart, an inability to reach or to be reached at deeper levels. It is also in midlife that we feel with poignancy that the most cherished institutions will not ultimately sustain us. Yet un-less we come to embrace this loneliness within our souls, we cut off avenues toward wholeness, both on the level of integrating oneself and on that of facilitating the growth of others. We have all seen young trees growing together in close proximity. For awhile they shelter and shade one another. But as they grow older, they begin to encroach on each other's space; we notice the malformations on the sides in contact. A painful pruning allows one tree to stand alone; as it ages, it fills out wholly, with fruitful branches in all directions. But the tree had to go through a pruning time of loneliness without the comfort-ing contact and reassurance of its closest neighbors.

It is customary to distinguish between loneliness and alone-ness. I am happily alone this afternoon as I write this meditation, but I am not at the moment lonely. People who distinguish between aloneness and loneliness urge us to foster the former because it aids self-discovery, and to banish the latter out of fear that it will lead to depression. But this is a serious error. For we must learn to encounter the pain and sadness associated with loneliness, because these difficult experiences can open up dimensions of our deepest being. We must feel these wounds to become healers of ourselves and others. In these matters, only the wounded physician heals. Painkillers, like distraction, diversion, and denial, on the level of the soul, hinder healing and new growth. Loneliness is not necessarily rejection or abandonment, which have the sense of direct actions by others toward us. But when that more subtle ache of loneliness enters consciousness, we should embrace it, in Ann Lindbergh's words, as "an angel of annunciation," for the pain is full of promise.

We are speaking, therefore, of loneliness as an experience that allows us to deepen and to expand our humanity, if we know how to become its companion. When we run away from this fellow traveler, we avoid our real feelings and try to nourish our spirits exclusively on the thin soup of rational reflection. Because we fear to experience the distress of dealing directly with our loneliness, we push it down into the neglected shadow corners of our psyche. We may think the problem finished, but it only festers in the dark, afflicting us in indirect and more dangerous ways. Yet the people of our time experience special difficulty in coping with their loneliness. In part, we are alienated from the natural world and from our own bodies; moreover, the haste and fragmentation of our relationships diminish neighborliness and community. We feel particularly isolated and even become aggressive to disguise the anxiety of our loneliness. If we develop a contempt for love and gentleness, it is frequently because we refuse to enter through the narrow portal of our own loneliness.

Creative artists and writers have learned to embrace their loneliness as a source of insight and empathy. Thomas Wolfe spoke for many creative spirits when he regarded loneliness as a condition of existence essential to creativity. Why is it important to suffer through some loneliness for a fuller life? Our loneliness puts us in touch with our true feelings, makes us sensitive to our real plight and our authentic needs. When we run away from our loneliness, we avoid the zone of our deepest feelings; we impoverish our spirits. In the guise of staying happy through diversions and constant company-seeking, we diminish joy in our lives because we alienate ourselves from our deeper longings. Loneliness is a yearning for contact with the deepest realms of ourselves. Our true feelings are pressed into the neglected shadow realms of our psyche.

We must not be naive in our praise of loneliness. Some people suffer mental damage from excessive isolation and neglect. In various personal and social ways, society victimizes many poor, elderly, homeless, and frail people. It would be cruel and thoughtless if we encouraged the oppressive circumstances of such persons by a blanket endorsement of loneliness. On the contrary, for those of us who are privileged with education and good material living standards, encounter with our own loneliness should make us more sensitive to the socially induced sufferings of poor and marginalized people. From our sensitivity to their condition, we will want to work for social and political change that would better their lot. Yet we can also learn from some poor and socially outcast persons who have worked through the pain of their own loneliness to become compassionate individuals with healthier priorities regarding material things and human needs. When we meet such individuals in shelters for the homeless, for example, we are touched and inspired by their profound humanity.

Loneliness can help us to make friends with our own deeper selves and to become richer friends to others. Wonder at the paradox: Through an encounter with loneliness we encounter authentic friendship. A further paradoxical reflection: It may well be that only in midlife and elderhood are we ready for the friendships, inward and outward, that result in the lessons of loneliness. For in earlier years our many active friendships may have been largely superficial associations for mere advantage or personal pleasure. Loneliness leads us along an arduous path to knowing who we really are. Only on this basis can genuine friendship be constructed. We are frequently estranged from our own deeper feelings and yearnings. Loneliness is an occasion for reintegrating these buried sentiments. We learn to love ourselves by allowing back into consciousness our wounded or repressed childhood, healthier parental images of self-nurture, and aged figures of inner wisdom. This inward community may enter only through some pain to our fearful and inflated ego.

In the end this archetypal community of inner friends provides an indispensable core for outward friendship. When the suffering of loneliness is experienced at the center of one's being, it grows outward into compassion, humor, and joy. Loneliness provides one of those few experiences in modern life when our distortions become transparent to us; in surrendering to the pain of this experience, we grow to our full stature. It is not loneliness that separates us from others, but the terror of a loneliness not fully embraced.

Put yourself in a place of quiet and solitude. It may be sitting in a park or by a body of water. Some may invoke feelings of loneliness on a walk through the woods. When your own feeling of loneliness arises, sit comfortably, close your eyes and breathe deeply, holding and slowly releasing your breath. (If you know how to induce a light state of trance through self-hypnosis – and you feel at ease with this condition – let it be the environment of this meditation.)

Begin by trying to identify the physical feelings of your loneliness. Is there pain in the region of the heart, or tightness in the throat or abdomen? Is it connected with a headache or muscle discomfort in the neck and shoulders? When you locate the place of this painfulness, imagine your breath flooding through the area of pain. You step back for a moment and observe the ebbing and flowing of your own life's breath making contact with the center of pain in this loneliness. Remind yourself as you wash through this pain that you are not running away from your reality, but rather that you are experiencing it fully at this very moment. You are not blocking the process; rather you are risking this involvement with loneliness in the faith that the process will carry you to the other side with greater self-knowledge and wisdom.

Envision your pain of loneliness as the center of a circle, a mandala-like image. Your consciousness in meditation encompasses the circle like a soothing, intertwining mist of intelligence and compassion. Now imagine that you are breathing through the center. How does it respond to the ebb and flow of your breath? Is there a special color or feeling associated with this focusing on the center of your loneliness? With each intake of breath, receive your loneliness. With each exhaling, surrender to its meaning for you. It may signify a longing to be united with God as the spiritual center of your being. The pain of loneliness becomes a necessary phase of separation from our usual distractions in order to encounter our yearning for divine presence within.

Finally, picture the center of your pain being transformed with healing energies radiating out to all parts of your being. Let this transformation take the form of compassion and friendship for others according to whatever images are appropriate in your life. These images may be specific individuals in your family or in other personal or occupational associations. What feelings, images, and thoughts arise? Take note of them. Picture with a sense of wonder the expanding circle of compassion as it radiates from the center of your loneliness. Let the enlarging rings of its movement take in areas of the world where violence and oppression are particularly acute. From the center of your own loneliness arise sentiments of justice, peace, and reconciliation.

5

FACING ABANDONMENT

If we are sensitive to the aging process, we can learn important lessons about our feelings and fears concerning abandonment. "Abandonment" is a very strong word that connotes an active rejection of another. Yet, although one can be abandoned or rejected intentionally, the sense of being abandoned can operate in quiet, even passive ways. The middle-aged woman, for example, may feel abandoned by her children as they go away to college or leave to establish new families. She might also experience subtle abandonment when her husband becomes increasingly absorbed in his work. Elderhood brings new encounters with feelings of abandonment. The death of long-time friends or of a spouse can arouse a severe sense of being left alone, even of being rejected. The post-retirement experience for many men convinces them that they have been cast aside by colleagues and institutions. Perhaps the deeper issue in post-retirement depression related to one's former job centers on abandonment. Persons speak of being useless or worthless; but underneath such considerations is the less-easily acknowledged sentiment of being abandoned by one's peers. Even more stark prospects of abandonment afflict elderly people in nursing homes. They feel rejected and cast off by members of their own families.

To appreciate why the sphere of being abandoned is so power-ful in our psyches, we must reflect on its origins in infancy. Our first human experience is that of intimate belonging in our mother's womb; before we can reflect on it, we have known in the most physical way total belonging, complete envelopment, and protective nurture. If we are fortunate in our earliest years, much of this caring, trust-creating environment continues. But it cannot and ought not continue as we first experienced it. We were bound to have experiences of childhood abandonment when we cried and parents did not immediately cater to our needs, or when they left our presence and we were not sure if they would return. Yet it was essential to our growth as separate personalities that we learned to negotiate the double-bind proc-ess of belonging and independence. These are risky waters to navigate for a healthy psychological balance. For parents can abandon us through neglect or rejection, but they can also "aban-don" that developing child's true personality through overcon-trol. The latter may be expressed by tyrannical dominance with direct fear of punishment or more subtly through lack of au-thentic attention to the emerging self of the child. In still other forms, the true personality of the child is "abandoned" by the parent who dominates by way of unstinting (and unrealistic) praise, as long as the child conforms to parental ideals and ex-pectations. When such individuals become adults, they may be unable or afraid to experience their true feelings. They may also turn a great deal of rage outward on others, displacing the anger they cannot recognize or risk as directed toward the original source of their abandonment.

Midlife and elderhood allow us to perceive, acknowledge, and own our encounters with abandonment. We can also understand how these experiences are played out in later life. We are able, perhaps for the first time, to see and appreciate our fears of not belonging and the consequences in our behavior toward inti-mates, friends, and associates. In youth we were either too close to the enchanting and overwhelming experiences of our earlier "abandonments" or too busy establishing our identities and roles to notice these deeper sources of our psychic makeup and malaise. By our middle years, we have had sufficient experience of the negative outcome of our fear of abandonment. We may realize, for example, that our excessive anger projected outward toward others, even intimate others, provides a clue to insecurity about our acceptance and our basic acceptability. We may be afraid that we are not lovable, that we don't belong, that others will abandon us. Still another sign of our fear of abandonment in midlife can manifest itself in a spirit of apathy, withdrawal, and resignation. We fear that if we make important changes in our attitudes and life-styles, we will become vulnerable to rejection. We become anxious that family, friends, and associates will distance themselves from us, opening up again our childhood terrors of abandonment. By meditating on our fears of abandonment and also on resources for counterbalancing this fear, we can approach our later years with increased understanding of ourselves and with courage to live more adventurously.

Place yourself in a quiet position for meditation and do a set of breathing exercises It is important to recapture in imagination concrete memories of abandonment. Some may be able to return to childhood scenes where the experience was vivid. Perhaps the death of a parent in your childhood or the separation of parents through divorce will revive feelings of abandonment. For others, childhood memories are too distant. If this is your situation, recall another traumatic event, perhaps the death or departure of a loved one, be it a spouse, parent, or friend. Many in our society have known the sense of being left behind or rejected through divorce. Let the painful memories well up again. Remember and picture where you were at the time; what job did you have? Such a setting of place can rekindle sentiments close to the actual feelings. This process will also activate indirectly your earliest fears of abandonment in childhood. Focus on one or two of these events, embracing again, without allowing too much sadness to enter your soul, the feeling of being excluded.

After you have dwelt some minutes on this experience, notice first of all that the pain can be borne. This already tells you something about your innate sources of strength. Even if you were to push the abandoment exercise into more extreme levels (for example, by gradually imagining the death or departure of all those closest to you) there would remain in you the power to sustain your life. You could open up again and reach out to others; moreover, you could learn to communicate more fully with archetypal voices within your own unconscious. These energies from your deepest self are like an inward community that understands you better than most outward individuals. In Jungian language some of these inner forces are called shadow or *anima* or *puer* or mother or *senex*. You are never abandoned by this inner congregation of psychospiritual elements. Some discover these inner powers through psychological reflection; others find them through contemplative dialogue with God within the soul. However these powerful inner-healing energies appear to you, embrace them as parts of your personal fellowship. These dimensions of you belong forever with you and you with them. If you can discover your inner family, outward experiences of abandonment cannot destroy you; on the contrary, the conscious events of rejection may lead you to make friends with your unconscious community.

As you dwell on how you are not abandoned ultimately by the spiritual forces of the cosmos, sense too how you are embraced by the unflagging tenderness and care of God. From a Christian perspective, we are participants in trinitarian life, in the divine community. Picture yourself enveloped by a warm, bright cloud of mystery. Within this cloud are the healing, energizing forces of your own deep psyche; see the whole cloud itself as part of a much larger realm of God's presence as a community. From a Jewish perspective, this communal aspect of divine presence flows from the experience of belonging to spiritual Israel. The strong organic sense of the Jewish people rests ultimately on this religious insight. You may also find this experience of nurturing fellowship by drawing to mind the actual persons from whom you experienced great benevolence or unconditional love during your life. Let these forces of love that have touched you personally become part of the mysterious congregation that moves gently and quietly through the cloud of blessing around you.

To discover again how much you belong to the world around and inside of you contributes to creative aging. On the one hand, you are able to empathize with the experience of abandonment in others because you too have gone through it. On the other hand, you can become a role model for others, revealing in your life the ability to rediscover community and wholeness beyond the crises of abandonment. Dwell in the concluding time of your meditation on abandonment experience as a catalyst for rediscovering deeper fellowship with nature, yourself, and other people. Imagine yourself growing older as a person of expanding care and benevolence, because you feel a greater communion with all creation. Try to see yourself perhaps twenty years from now — older, grayer, but also a richer human being who belongs to all the world in a caring way. If you can see your own face in these later years, imagine it as though waves of benevolence ripple forth from it to embrace all beings near and far. As an elder you have become in your very body-person a healer of the devastating fear of abandonment because you have transcended its terror to experience a new mode of belonging to all.

6

REMEMBERING OURSELVES

Our aging process creates our story. People, events, successes and failures, joys and sorrows shape our individual tales. By midlife or elderhood we should be able to craft our memories into a number of stories. "Life Review" has become a very useful technique for helping older people get in touch with both positive and negative aspects of their personal history. Even the negative dimensions, the injuries since childhood, become agents for growth as we confront and work through them. Yet we associate a type of reminiscing with an elderhood that presents itself as rather sad and boring. We say of such people that they live in the past, making anyone within earshot an audience for endless monologues on the past. Occasionally a sterling raconteur can keep our attention, but usually we want to escape. The problem lies not in the stories, but rather in their lack of connectedness to life now. Recollection of one's past expresses this difference. We tell stories, gather up important aspects of the past in a twofold way. Recollection honors and recreates the past, but unlike reminiscing, it applies the past to the present and to the future. When an elder tells a story in this way, we sense that he/she is also alive in the present, that the past is speaking to present and future concerns. Let us meditate further on getting in touch with our stories in this sense of recollecting.

Remembering constitutes one of the marvels of being alive. As the same persons over time, we are able to preserve the past; we know its hurts, but we can also relive its memories of love. Recalling our past is a form of autobiography; the narratives of our experience form the warp and woof of personal identity and integrity. But as we tell stories in midlife and elderhood, we continually shape them into new forms. We can never go home again, as it were, and see the events with our twelve-year-old eyes. But this reshaping of past happenings doesn't necessarily mean distorting these events. Rather we may see new meanings in the earlier happenings both as past occasions and as symbols that aid us in fashioning our own futures. Healthy reminiscing, which is not lost in the past, provides the continuity that helps us maintain self-esteem with a sense of connected identity, and allows us to cope with losses that might otherwise be sources of excessive depression. Let us move directly into a meditation on recollecting our stories.

Begin your meditation on recollection by contacting your past through memories. Place yourself in a comfortable place, perhaps in your customary spot for contemplation, and do the breathing exercises with eyes closed. It could be helpful in this meditation to have looked at a family album just before beginning, or perhaps you have a toy or other object from your childhood that can be a focal point for attention and recollection. Recall the house in which you grew up; see its rooms again, the other persons who dwelled in it, how they moved about and what they did. Perhaps you can remember colors and distinctive smells; did the house have a yard and what went on there? When you have sufficiently established yourself in the old context, think about your grandparents, if they lived nearby, and also imagine your parents as they were in your childhood. Remember them as explicitly as possible: how they dressed, what they would say, what activities occupied their time. Did you have any special feelings about older persons when you were a child? Did your parents, who were probably middle-aged at the time, have any particular opinions about aging? Did the surrounding culture give any messages about aging? We can ask ourselves if our parents had any notions of developing their full potential all through the aging process, or whether adulthood was simply a plateau where one remained generally the same.

Focus on your parents individually. Did your mother reveal particular fears about aging as a woman in our culture? Perhaps your parents saw themselves as already old in early midlife; what would this mean concerning their own self-understanding? Was there any challenge to your mother's self-esteem because of aging? Did role reversal take place between father and mother in any noticeable way, or did they continue through midlife and elderhood with the same roles? How might such fixed roles have influenced their ability to express certain feelings and desires? How did your father relate to his work? Perhaps his occupation was a source of encouragement to him, or it could have had very negative results on his personality. Was he mostly defined by his work and totally enveloped in it to the exclusion of other things? Or perhaps your father's attitude toward work was more balanced than the driven spirit of today's overachievers. What do you remember about the relationship between father and mother over a long span of years? Did they grow apart or closer together during their aging process? Ask yourself if this change had anything to do with aging itself. Do you have any memory of institutions, e.g., churches, social agencies, that were concerned about aging when you were young? What are your recollections about visiting homes for the elderly?

These moments of quiet reflection on your family raise up memories of how this particular network of past relationships influenced you. It is useful to think about how you resemble your parents in your own aging process and also how you differ. This immersion in the concrete context of your history will also bring back memories of special care and love manifested toward you. If some of these positive sentiments arise, embrace them and let them linger in you as sustaining recollections. But this journey backward into your early life may also elicit memories of unhealed injuries in you from those past periods. This brief meditation cannot deal adequately with the burdens of the past;

the latter need time and possibly the aid of a counselor. But contemplation of your past may help you formulate and reexperience problems that need to be unblocked for your own creative aging. It could be particularly helpful to record such insights or unresolved problems in a personal journal for future coping with these issues. Just as working with dreams can enlighten and strengthen your developing psyche, so also autobiographical musings in a meditative ambience can trigger important clues for your own individuation process.

By getting in touch with your memories, you set the stage for considering your attitudes toward aging in the present and toward the future. Remember our earlier point about the difference between reminiscing and recollecting; we said that the value of the latter was how it carried the past into conversation with present and future development. If you are now a young person, reflect on your present attitudes toward aging. How is this expressed in terms of feelings toward your own parents? What comes to mind when you think about visiting nursing homes or other institutions of the elderly? Do you easily fall into stereotypical views about being old, perhaps in humorous ways? Do you have any special feelings about sexual relations among the elderly? Would you enjoy spending a weekend with an old person or possibly taking a trip with one?

If you are now in middle age, the reflections on aging in your own family may elicit more poignant feelings about getting older. Let yourself sense whatever messages come to you in the present; perhaps you recognize the irretrievable loss of youth with its seemingly unrestricted potentials. You may already have encountered some severe challenges, such as illness or divorce, that remind you of your limits and mortality. It could be that you notice yourself repeating negative patterns of your own parents as they aged; for example, this might be expressed by the way in which you handle your anger. Yet this awareness about adopting the habits of your parents can also become an occasion for changing the observed behavior.

Memories of your family could also evoke recollections about your occupation in midlife. Have you fallen into a rut of apathy and boredom in your job, as though you were trapped in a meaningless pursuit, with little hope of change before retirement? Can you imagine how your work could become part of your own development as a person, as well as a contribution to the welfare of others? Have your recollections of the past keyed any thoughts about your relationships with those closest to you? Perhaps difficulties or failures in marital relationships have affected your attitudes about aging. Do you put time into cultivating friendships as an increasingly valuable dimension of growing older? It may also be that your memories about the very old people in your childhood arouse feelings about your responsibilities toward your own frail and very elderly parents.

If you are already in the time of elderhood, memories of how people aged in your youth could be a source for dealing with your own attitudes now toward the proximity of death and toward the disabilities of elderhood. In the face of some of these threats, is elderhood becoming a time of depression and escape into the past? Or are you able to cope positively with the fears and deficiencies of old age, working through them toward worthwhile results for you and others? If encouraging thoughts arise on this matter, let them stay with you for a while as sources of inspiration. Is your elderhood a lonely march to the periphery of society, or are you coming back to the center of things in your interests and activities? How might you be taking on some of the broader concerns of humanity where you actually live? Perhaps you can make specific for yourself at this point one other involvement for peace or justice or ecological improvement.

The purpose of this meditation is to turn fruitless reminiscing into valuable recollection. How can you find lessons from your own past to instruct and encourage you on the journey toward greater wholeness? A variety of sad and joyful feelings could surge through you as you gather together again the neglected memories about aging in your own life story. As you sit quietly in the concluding moments of this contemplation, summarize in your mind the most striking images from this exercise, whether they seem negative or positive. Such images contain energy for you; you can work on them again in meditation and in your journal.

·7

RECLAIMING NATURE

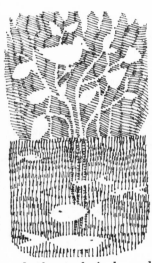

A new appreciation of our place in the natural world gives us valuable insights into our own aging. Many aspects of our lives conspire to alienate us from the rhythm of nature. In recent centuries especially, we have benefitted wonderfully from science and technology. Great cities with sophisticated cultures have sprung up. We soar through the air and speed down highways with machines of our own invention. Everywhere we look our daily lives are surrounded by the marvels of scientific research and its applications: computers, radiology, lasers, electronic communications, and other technical wonders – the list of these impressive achievements could cover pages.

Yet for all its genius, our modern way of life has orphaned humans from their roots in mother earth. We have come to see ourselves as a species apart from the natural world from which we evolved. We associate ourselves with the realm of history and culture. We relegate the nonhuman world to nature, as if it were a foreign sphere. We go so far as to picture nature as our enemy because it seems to threaten our lives with its rhythms of decline, death, and transformation. Why can't we be like the machines and electronic devices of our own creation: enduring, relatively permanent and deathless? Much longevity literature seems driven by such a question.

What does separation from nature have to do with our aging? It fosters in our psyches an anxiety-ridden attitude of denying our own natural seasons and their eventual ending. Moreover, our anti-nature mentality causes us to become callous toward the needs and the beauty of the earth and its other creatures. We tend to age in a warring posture against the matrix of our spiritual and physical ecology. We have reflected on the scientific and technological motivators of our anti-nature attitudes, but let us consider other equally important teachers of our alienation from the ecosystem. It is not only science but more importantly the humanities that inculcate a self-defeating enmity toward the natural world.

The preponderance of Western religious, philosophical and literary works corroborate our hostility against the lessons of nature. Consider some central examples from Christianity as it has been popularly taught for millenia. The message of Christmas and Easter is that a redeemer like ourselves saves us from the ravages of nature, connected with both spiritual death (the pagan, nature religions were supposedly incapable of altering sinful human ways) and physical death through the pledge of resurrected, eternal life. This vision, despite contemporary theological attempts to correct it, is still ingrained in popular piety and culture. To a considerable extent, religions and philosophies, as products largely of our own longings for life eternal, tell us what we want to hear. It is extremely hard for humans to work maturely through the prospects of their own diminishment, decline, and death. We "naturally" cry out for saviors from Jesus to Sun Myung Moon who will promise us eternal life.

Two corrective points need to be made: The yearning for life eternal need not lead us to an anti-ecological view; moreover, to sentimentalize or romanticize nature has its own pitfalls. Mystics from Francis of Assissi to Teilhard de Chardin were able to increase their love for the natural order precisely because they envisioned it as an integral part of the divine plan. Brother Ass and Sister Moon became our close kin; Teilhard's evolutionary vision conceived nature transformed and cherished in God's Omega stage. It is interesting that these minority perspectives in the West derive from meditation on the natural world (Francis) and on a scientific contemplation of the world (Teilhard). Romanticizing nature, however, can become still another form of escaping the hard prospects of our own finitude. Such an attitude sentimentalizes nature as though suffering and sorrow were excluded from the experience of the animal realm. This Pollyanna mentality beguiles us with false comfort about our own place in the earth's system; failure and pain become unreal to us. Furthermore, the sentimentalist of this sort fails to empathize deeply with the tragic aspects of all creation. He or she might also oppose even the wise and respectable scientific investigations of nature.

Nature can teach us to find peace in our limited life span; we are her products, enjoy her blessings, contribute to her future, and make room by our leave-taking for her other children. Nature instructs us in the bittersweet life. We empathize with her tragic face, the pain and suffering of her creatures. We become more sensitized to the requirements of the ecosystem with its myriad and often delicate interconnections. If we understand in depth our solidarity with the lot of the seas, forests, weather systems, and our animal kin, we stand a better chance to form and live out a just and caring morality toward fellow humans. Alienation from nature becomes the forerunner of enmity toward those of other creeds, mores, and ideologies. We erect hard walls of difference rather than bridges of continuity. If we could all become convinced that our human enemies from all sides are primarily children of nature, sharing her lot and responsible for her future, we might evoke the good will needed for the establishment of peace with justice.

A meditation on nature is not a superfluity. It is an essential contemplation for creative aging with important ethical ramifications. Thoreau knew this connection in his experience at Walden; Emerson felt a transcending link with the natural realm that lifted him to mystic appreciation; Muir understood our union with wilderness as a rejuvenation of spirit.

✳

Place yourself in a comfortable outdoor place, perhaps a garden or a park. Close your eyes and breathe deeply and slowly, holding your breath for a time, then releasing it. As you do this, get in touch with the simple but all-important fact that your very existence depends from moment to moment on drawing in, chemically altering, and expelling air from the natural surrounding. Experience this constant process, how intrinsically involved you already are with the environment. Notice the sun's rays lighting up things around you; rather than take it all for granted, dwell admiringly on the sun's work of illumination, warmth, and transformation. Remember how completely dependent we are on this star for all life on earth. Think, too, of the wonderful process of your own sight, the complex visual organs and their dependence on light. From middle age onward, we are in an especially fertile time for exploring the hidden depths of our own consciousness. Reflect on how our connection with nature is both physical and psychic. We carry in our bodily makeup mineral traces from the earliest formative explosions of the planet. In this sense we are as old as the mountains and the seas; we are physically one with the stuff of the universe.

As you close your eyes and concentrate again on your breathing, think of your body as a wonderfully complex creation of the earth, intimately linked with this matrix, but also independent from it in your reflective and self-determining powers. Yet even your intelligent consciousness is an offspring of nature. We do not understand fully the mystery of the mind's evolution, but we should be able to appreciate our affliation with all brain-led creatures. Moreover, the deeper psychic energies (archetypal forces in Jungian language) that appear as images in dreams and in other symbolic, artistic modes call for our attention. We are beckoned to enter into dialogue with these inner images and symbols. By being more consciously in touch with these forces of the unconscious through dreams and other symbolic artistic modes, we grow in the understanding of ourselves and of the natural realm from which all these marvels spring. Through our conversation with – and sometimes painful encounter with – these archetypal energies, we move toward a greater completion of the evolutionary process in ourselves. Let your meditative imagination embrace whatever images come to you of this physical and psychic process of nature alive within yourself.

Let your meditation conclude on the significance of greater compassion with the finite world. As we work through the transitions of midlife and elderhood we become more fully aware of our own finitude and mortality. If we can become compassionate toward the similar lot of fellow humans, of animals, and other sentient creatures as well as all other forms of existence, we can learn to love the world. From this vantage point of compassion, call before your imaginative screen those you have learned to see as your enemies. Without denying your important differences with these "enemies," be they persons, animals, or other entities, focus on your common linkages with nature: how we all spring from the womb of earth, how we require similar sustenance from nature, and how among more complex beings we need affection, cooperation, and respect. Let us age as ever more compassionate children of our parenting earth and become models of empathy for younger people.

·8

ENCOUNTERING MIDLIFE

Midlife doesn't permit easy definitions in terms of beginning and ending. We can speak of a general period in a typical full life span between youth and old age or elderhood. Given longer life expectancy, the period between forty and sixty seems adequate for our purposes. Certain characteristic happenings during this time are much more valuable for understanding middle age than mere matters of chronology. In this meditation we want to outline briefly some of these challenging traits and to describe concrete steps that midlife persons can take toward creative aging.

The chief awareness underlying many problems in middle age concerns death; not death in general, but specifically our own process of dying and our final demise. Unlike the more generic assessments of young people concerning morality, we come to sense experientially our death. We know we are middle-aged when we find ourselves counting the years from the end rather than from the beginning. We are quite willing to give a count from birth, but the counting that matters, that has a value potential for us, numbers the years before our inevitable decline. Some find this connection between midlife and death awareness to be morbid and exaggerated. Put the morbidity aside for a moment; as we will insist later on, positive uplifting results from confronting finitude. But do we exaggerate by claiming personal death insights as central to midlife issues?

The language surrounding contemporary discussions of middle age may avoid the bluntness of death-talk, but in fact it focuses on physical and psychological mortality. We find references to a restricted sense of time or to realizing a loss of youthfulness. Some try to restore the feelings of youth by athletic endeavors in middle age; others pursue new romances. Still others dispay anger at the young, criticizing their immaturity. Sometimes this critique is warranted, but often it merely displays envy of the young for their very youth — and their distance from death. When the middle-aged show hostility toward the old, they may be hiding fears about their own declining years. Forms of psychological dying also appear during this period. The myths by which we lived in childhood and youth may lose their energizing force. The death of these waking dreams about what constitutes a happy, successful future may plunge us into reflections on finitude. It may shock us into revising the strong lines with which we pattern the canvas of our remaining time of life. For those more sensitively in touch with their unconscious life, dreams disclose similar themes about mortality and the need to launch out in new directions.

These considerations emphasize that midlife demands a fresh awareness of a new situation. It is more than a mere continuation of youth, as though life after the voting age were a plateau of homogeneous adulthood. New questions challenge our past ways; long-neglected issues from the deeper reaches of the psyche clamor for attention. We cannot resolve these matters with mechanical efficiency as though they were a technological problem. For we are facing deeper, complex issues that defy quick solutions. Yet these very challenges become the doorways through which we can set out on a new journey toward realizing our own wholeness. A trip must begin with the first steps taken now or we remain standing on old ground. If the crises of midlife are to become "angels of annunciation," we must be willing to follow behind wise spiritual guides. Let us look at a few steps in this venture that can become for us an adventure of discovery.

Since many of the midlife issues derive from a confrontation with our own mortality, we could begin by exploring concretely these related matters. Some may wish to start with readings that stimulate reflection. A direct approach would be to investigate the now abundant literature on death and dying, as well as books in philosophy, religion, and psychology that center on this topic. We may, however, find an indirect avenue through biography or high-quality fiction; this can be more gripping and interest-sustaining. The lives of inspiring figures show us how crucial midlife transitions were made; they also encourage us to hope that our own crossings-over will have positive results.

Still another way to begin the process in private consists in meditative journal-keeping. The two elements, a period of contemplation and journal-writing, can sustain each other. We may be more inclined to set aside times for meditation if we have committed ourselves to putting our thoughts in journal form. And the writing process itself will stimulate further reflections and new insights beyond what we knew in the meditation proper. The simple meditation techniques in these exercises could be employed in conjunction with journal-reflection. The reading mentioned above will also engender ideas for the journal. Reflective autobiography should be more than diary-type notations about everyday events. The deeper questions with their special emotions must be addressed.

The reflective journal can be greatly enhanced by recording and learning from our dreams. This rich but perplexing area will usually require the aid of some instructional literature and possibly a guide or a group situation of exploration. Dreams represent a storied playground of the mind when it is not under close direction of our waking ego. In the relaxed time of sleep, the imagination gives us symbols and dramas with important clues for self-understanding. When we learn to decipher some of these mysterious images, we perceive various fears or conflictual situations with tensions that reveal hidden aspects of our mental and emotional functioning. The affective or feeling tone surrounding the dream story becomes particularly important as a manifestation of our unconscious needs and desires. In addition to disclosing our inner struggles, dream work can indicate paths toward psychospiritual wholeness. Dreams thus become healing and reconciling instruments for the wounds of the soul and open avenues for personality growth. For two reasons, midlife offers an especially rich field for dream exploration. First, we have been sufficiently tried and tempered by life in order to acknowledge our psychological dysfunctions and our need for deeper, worthier modes of living. Secondly, our ego identity is well enough established to sustain the hard scrutiny of dream analysis without defensively resisting the process. Our longer history itself will provide valuable symbolic disclosures of how to relate to self, others, and to the natural world.

This willingness to undertake a voyage of self-discovery in middle age prepares us to take new outward steps toward successful aging. We will feel free to educate ourselves about personal and social dimensions of aging. We may be in positions with business, professional, social, and religious institutions to promote educational programs on aging at all levels. We will become interested in our local situation relative to the aging population, its demographics, living standards, and special needs. We will want to know about the quality of services and about various centers for the aging, beginning in our own region. Do enough quality programs exist in education and counseling about aging, as well as in services for older people? We will become concerned not only with the educational needs of the middle-aged, but also with the plight of the elderly. In this realm, involvements can take us in many directions: health care, nutritional services, protection of legal rights, transportation needs, and secure living environments for the old. As our concrete awareness grows, we will become concerned also about the confined elderly, especially those who are frail or abused. Perhaps our own situation as middle-aged children of frail, elderly parents will alert us to the unique problems of this large group. But freed from our fear and denial of aging, we will be willing to befriend the old who, because of their disabilities, may have been rejected by us in the past.

This change of attitude in midlife can launch us into an even broader transformation of personal priorities. Concern for the needs of aging groups awakens us to a fuller awareness of our social vocation in middle age. We realize the summons to become servants of universal human issues; we are undergoing a transition of enlightenment from our narrow, private goals of youth toward engagement in wider human values. The call is away from a form of self-centeredness without self-scrutiny toward a new self-concept, sparked by our inward journey, that causes us to become increasingly citizens of the whole earth with its special needs. Creative elderhood begins with these transitions of middle age toward developing a universal spirit in oneself. The immediate needs of our families and other commitments of daily life remain as major responsibilities for us. But if we are truly growing into fullness of age, we will seek out particular social causes that support peace, justice, and human dignity.

These may be local involvements such as programs for needy children, for the homeless, for the impoverished, the sick, or the imprisoned. One's social engagement may focus on ecological questions regarding various forms of pollution, from toxic wastes to nuclear power dangers. Others may choose to concentrate on issues of human rights around the world through organizations like Amnesty International. Still others will address matters of domestic and international violence, searching out and promoting plans for resolving conflicts. The field of such involvement stands wide open. What matters is not an intellectual assessment only, but individual commitment to a few carefully chosen causes. Maturity in midlife does not permit the idealistic discouragement of many youths: If we cannot make a perfect world, we will take no steps toward a better one. For those who have undergone the conversions of middle age, these social involvements are no longer a question of arbitrary choice, but rather an intrinsic part of one's calling toward an elderhood of wholeness and universality.

Let your breathing exercises with their slow, rhythmic cadence carry you inward to the deeper sources of your physical life. As you breathe, imagine the wonderful inward articulation of lungs gathering oxygen, of the heart moving nutritional blood to your cells, and veins carrying exhausted blood back for replenishment. These and other systems are marvelously programed with the intricacies of your brain and nervous systems. Just as you need to go inward to find yourself physically, so too you must take an inner journey in middle age to discover your psychospiritual self. The articulations of this spiritual/mental personality are just as complex as the bodily ones. The inner bodily motions give you a special clue to a central problem of your spiritual existence in midlife. What a splendid network of bodily workings sustains life moment by moment over against death. Now that the illusions of youthful immortality have passed, the inward journey confronts you with the basic midlife experience of personal finitude and mortality. You are now going to face the issue without wavering, because you know that creative aging for you depends on working through this key dilemma.

The road inward does not lead to a dead end, however. As you start listening to neglected voices speaking from your subterranean unconscious, you gradually gain courage to let go of your fears of death. For these voices speak convincingly of a sustaining benevolence and an ultimate beauty of the love in which you were conceived. These inner utterances are frequently experienced as spontaneous insights that spring to mind in ways that seem to be beyond ordinary intelligence. As you exhale, let yourself go with trust into the same supporting environment of truth and love. In these inward springs you will drink the waters of courage and hope. With this help, you will pass through the trials of midlife, purified for and opened up to an expanding creativity as you age.

As you dwell on these reflections, let your imagination form a silhouette of yourself moving through an inner tunnel. As you approach life at the tunnel's end, your newly transformed body-person image grows larger. Just as the lighted exit becomes bigger as you near it, so the silhouetted, transparent image of you expands. As you go out from the inward tunnel into the light of the world, you notice how your expansive being wants and is able to embrace the struggling, suffering world with a new spirit of compassion and commitment. Before you journeyed within, your body-person was smaller, more physically confined, protecting itself, boosting itself against a menacing world. Now in midlife your whole being has found release to love and serve the world with a more universal spirit. This spirit will be contagious for others.

As you end your contemplation, remind yourself that you can always return to those inner wellsprings of enlightened strength. Choose one social cause that strikes you as particularly worthy of involvement. Focus on this issue; let its scenes unfold on the screen of your imagination. When you feel sufficiently in touch with this social problem, visualize again your expanded self as it emerged from the tunnel. This spiritualized image of you walks toward the problematic area. You are realistic about its complexities, offering no magic solutions. But your image can now empathize deeply with the suffering or perilous situation as you search for positive steps of reconciliation. The issue may remain unsolvable for a long time, but you perceive a change in yourself. You are aging with a more humane and expansive spirit as you walk from midlife toward elderhood. The inward path leads you outward with renewed vision and commitment.

·9

PREPARING FOR ELDERHOOD

It is hard to grow old in a society geared to the young. Certain physical diminishments of older people would be hard to bear. But an ageist culture imposes further psychic injuries on the elderly. Although many enjoy good health into their seventies and eighties, many other elders experience new disabilities or the aggravation of chronic illnesses. Here we need to distinguish between the independent and active elderly who try to cope with infirmities, and the large number of confined, frail, unwell old people. Among those over sixty, the first group surely represents the great majority, but the latter segment of the elderly population is significantly growing. We do not want to forget them in a realistic meditation on old age. As we examine positive options for the old, we cannot ignore the fact that serious disabilities, sometimes accompanied by pain and fatigue, incline us to narrow our horizons, to lose interest in life. Our physical wellbeing strongly affects our mental outlook. Besides the actual disabilities themselves, the fear of incurring grievous losses, such as those of memory and bodily self-control, weighs on the minds of the old. On a lesser but not unimportant level, just looking aged and infirm can have serious psychological consequences for some people.

Beyond these vital issues of health, the old experience other significant losses. Friends and associates fall ill and die; the loss of a spouse can profoundly alter one's attitude toward life. The new proximity of one's own death often depresses people, especially those who suppressed or avoided encountering this phenomenon in middle life. Obituary notices continually remind the old of the death of their contemporaries, persons whose passing portends their own demise. Added to these burdens, retirement from an active work life still makes too many older people feel useless, unworthy, and rejected. This, unfortunately, is still so frequently the case that the topic of retirement, of association of self-respect with an occupational role, deserves a separate meditation. For many people, retirement also brings with it financial worries in an unstable economy. With more time for reminiscing, we ask whether our past involvements have been worth the years put into them. Discouragement settles on an older person when it appears that goals were not accomplished, or if they were achieved, may not have been of real value. For such people, this sense of failure carries a special dimension: They feel that they can no longer redeem the time by starting a new venture. They may even be tormented by a considerable sense of guilt because they believe the time was not used wisely in the past. They resign themselves to a half-life of puttering around without lively interests and without any zest for adventure.

If the above picture seems bleak, we insist that it is essential to dwell on these negative realities of elderhood. It will do us no good to move into contemplation of old age in an unrealistic manner. If there are steps now that we can take toward creative elderhood, they must proceed from a realistic vision of aging's challenge. When we study elders who learned to grow through and beyond diminishments, we find that they squarely faced the challenge of age. They experienced limits of health and fortune, yet were able to expand the quality time left to them for their own development and for the benefit of others. They knew firsthand the downward physical slope, aggravated by cultural stereotypes that further abuse the old. Yet they transformed this descent into a spiritual and humanistic ascent.

The experience of diminishments can become a school for

humility and truth. Humility is not the self-deprecation and de-spair mentioned above; rather, this virtue represents a lived understanding of how things really are. On one side, humility rejects illusory self-inflation, that futile effort by which we give ourselves immortality and elevate ourselves over others. On the other hand, humility is the sister of truth because she cures us of false expectations about life. Thus a humble person is also a grateful individual. Instead of decrying the world for not ful-filling our false expectations, he or she gives thanks for all bless-ings in this beautiful but limited existence. Truthfulness permits such people to encounter the prospect of their death without exaggerated fear and diversionary denial.

When elders embrace the truth about themselves, they do not retreat from the world because it is imperfect or has treated them unfairly. The elder of humble truth can speak out and act with risky courage against injustices and other evils in the world, for he or she no longer puts stock in fleeting honors and unreal expectations. There are no longer any bets to hedge. This truthful elder, moreover, is in a position to counsel others with wisdom. Furthermore, when we have become more humble/truthful in age's school of diminishments, we can empathize sincerely with the mental and physical pain of others, because we know this pain in our own person. This empathy heightens respect for self and for others. We respect others when we honor their value as independent and diverse beings; we can foster their welfare without making them tools for our own untruthful ambitions.

The elderly person of humble truth, taught by the wisdom of diminishments, can also open up to a more intense life of com-passionate care for the wider community of humankind. This is a high ideal of elderhood: to become more honest within in order to reach out to others with altruistic care. Such a vision of old age rejects the modern stereotype of older people withdrawing into private pursuits only, leaving the great social needs of humankind to younger generations. On the contrary, the truly spiritual elder loves the world in all its dimensions from the most sensual to the most intellectual. He and she are now able to be compassionate with the human race and the earth itself, because they experience in their aging persons both the limits and the promise of existence. Moreover, the care they exercise is more altruistic, since they have made peace with their own finitude. They no longer need to use the world to bolster their egos and defend them against mortality. Thus such elders will take steps to return to the centers of great conflictual issues: war/peace, hunger/nourishment, injustice/justice, prejudice/reconciliation, ignorance/education.

Many exemplary models of such an elderhood can be found, such as that of the black educator Benjamin Mays or the pacifist social worker Dorothy Day, or the theologian-physician Albert Schweitzer. Yet this ideal of a compassionate, caring elder, embracing the suffering world with wisdom and unselfishness, must not be confined to celebrities who contributed to the solution of major social problems. The very same spirit of an elderhood for the world can be manifested in quiet and unsung ways. For example, the older person of limited energies who tutors a less-privileged minority child or who writes a letter for the release of a prisoner of conscience – such a one exemplifies the elderly vocation toward ever greater compassion and care. Examples of this attitude can be multiplied indefinitely; what counts is grasping its essential spirit.

If the above description of inward spirituality embracing the world is an authentic master theme for elderhood, what steps toward it can begin now? Most of the points made in the previous meditation about middle age are also applicable to older persons. Some of those are reading, meditation, journal-keeping, reflection groups, and social-service involvements. But elderhood with its particular challenges calls for certain appropriate steps to realize the visions sketched above toward inner and outer development. Education and counseling for retirement would be especially helpful for the elderly. These programs allow a retiree to review in an organized way the emotional and social problems of leaving the workplace after many years of making one's job milieu a principal activity. Special counseling for individuals and families entering the retirement period can open up new avenues for refocusing skills and interests. Such advising, whether done individually or in group-therapy sessions, will also explore the new network of relations within the family caused by retirement from one's traditional work role. Husbands and wives will want to rethink and agree upon new ways of dividing their domestic and outside functions. For example, an elderly woman, who may have raised a family and spent years actively supporting her husband's career, may desire to seek more direct involvements of her own outside the home. Other adjustments may arise from altered financial standing after retirement or from certain health limitations. Therefore, the ideal sketched above for a more creative elderhood must be shaped within the framework of a new setting surrounding retirement. The motivating vision will remain an abstraction unless it is adapted to the real circumstances of each elderly person.

Once these aspects of personalizing the vision according to individual needs, talents, and interests is understood, other steps can be taken to foster structures of empowerment for the elderly. Some may choose to work for improving institutions that promote a better quality of life for old people. Such organizations could be senior centers where a broad range of educational and social programs is offered in conjunction with schools that may already have a significant curriculum in gerontology. Those who appreciate the value of psychological counseling and reflection groups for the elderly will invest energy to create opportunities in this most important area for new meaning, hope, and enthusiasm in later life. Elderly church people can examine how well religious institutions are ministering with and to the elderly. Are the churches, which should be particularly sensitive to the needs of the elderly poor, using facilities and other resources to serve old people? Are Christian and Jewish institutions incorporating the elderly at every level of ministry, worship, administration, and service? The confined, frail, and disabled elderly are particularly in need of care. Sometimes this takes the form of various material support systems, but just as vital is continued friendship and caring for these persons.

Beyond direct service to the elderly lies an inexhaustible field of options by which older persons can realize an elderhood for the world. If they have been seized and motivated by the ideal

of elderhood as a time for sharing wisdom and for compassionate service, older people can work in numerous ways to make
concrete in the world their deepest moral and ethical convictions. This central vocation of old age will be embodied in many
modes: working for the betterment of racial relations, for the
preservation of human rights around the world, and for the
elimination of nuclear weapons. These are but a few examples
of many crucial and valuable involvements for the good of humankind. To take steps in old age toward such goals brings to
full flowering our potential for human development.

Begin to contemplate this topic by first doing breathing exercises in a suitable quiet place. As you complete about ten such
breathing motions, picture yourself as an elderly individual,
whether or not you actually are such. The point is to imagine
yourself as an elder with appropriate changes in hair color and
facial formation. Perhaps your step is a little slower and you are
not quite as erect in posture as you once were. You are close to
or past retirement; you desire to concentrate your meditative
attention on the most creative options for you as an older person.
Three moments of this meditation interlace with one another to
form a dynamic whole: real encounter, inward growth, and outward dedication. It is not a matter of going from one to the
other in a linear way; rather all three moments interrelate with
creative tension at all times.

Focus again quietly on the rhythmic pattern of your breathing. For a few minutes put aside any words and images that
naturally come into your mind. As much as possible concentrate
on your breathing process; notice the bodily changes such as
the extension of your chest and abdomen with inhaling and
exhaling. Be gently aware of physical sensations, the rush of
breath pulled in and let out, the sound of your breathing, and
perhaps even muscular discomforts or pressures as you sit. This
"empty mind" exercise for some minutes will lead you through
your habitual ego defenses of rational conceptions. As you
move beyond these mental constructs, you will be disposed to

encounter the deeper voices of your soul as you turn to the three moments of this contemplation.

When you are ready, imagine again the elderly you facing the most fearful and challenging loss of elderhood. For some this may be loss of a spouse; for others, certain physical or social disabilities. Let whatever comes to you dwell deeply in your quieted consciousness; hold the images without struggling against them even if they are upsetting. The disconcerting losses of elderhood may seem to be too negative a way of beginning this mediation. Yet this first phase represents an essential moment of truth for you; you are allowing the hard reality of your finiteness and limitations to overcome the illusory fantasies by which we hide from truth. The reality of our condition draws us inward to seek sources of strength and renewal.

The second moment of the meditation, that of inwardness, has already begun by moving beyond the outer layer of restless thoughts and allowing the reality of your condition to grasp you imaginatively. You are ready now to embrace with humility the inner lessons that teach you the truth about yourself. By serious listening you will eventually hear hitherto unheard voices from your inner being assuring you that you have started to journey on the right path. As you sit in the presence of your fears about old age, these enemies become your friends. At some point they will take you by the hand and lead you to the only truth that can free you from paralyzing fear and foster empathy for yourself and for others. A new awareness of respect for all life will emerge and draw you outward to social/ethical dedication.

During the third moment, imagine the elderly you standing in a high place with arms outstretched in a gesture of welcome. Because you are less deluded about and more empathetic toward the world, you can take new steps to embrace individuals and groups in their various social needs. This is not a naïve love of humanity without critical discernment. You know better than ever that all universal human problems are complex; you must scrutinize well before venturing into the great issues of peacemaking with justice and the cultivation of human rights. But you are convinced now that you were not given the gift of elderhood for private pleasures only. The process of your aging has brought you to the last and greatest summons of your life. You will heed the call now to find ways to share the wisdom, skills, and love that radiate from you. You understand that as you give of yourself to others in the last phase of life, the blessings multiply in the sharing.

LIVING TRUTHFULLY

"Truth-full-ness": Becoming full of truth as one ages is a particularly worthy topic of meditation. So many forces are at work in society to cause us to distort or cover up the reality of things. Even before we have arrived at a firm sense of self-identity and discernment, we are loaded down with untruths. In our earliest years parents may, with seemingly good intentions, tell us lies about others in the family or in the neighborhood. Or these major figures of our childhood teach us hypocrisy by speaking one way and acting in another. No doubt such parents are usually only repeating patterns of falsehood that they learned from their own social milieu. Moreover, they may deal in untruths out of their own fears and insecurities; to face reality steadfastly requires considerable courage. But whatever the motives of these formative figures, they leave us immersed in a sea of falsehood about many aspects of life. The familial lessons in dissimulation and twisted outlooks are all too frequently corroborated by community prejudices. By a kind of social osmosis, we are educated in a cluster of prejudices toward other groups. Some are despised for their racial component; others are opposed for their religious beliefs; still others display ethnic differences or are described as enemies threatening our survivial.

Little wonder, then, that becoming a person of truth is a lifetime task; there is so much to unlearn about ourselves and
others by the time we reach youthful maturity. If we are fortunate in our associations and our education in young adulthood,
we can shed some of the more destructive unrealities instilled in
us. But the twenties, thirties, and even forties remain years of
existing by alien codes for the majority of people. We want to
succeed according to parental aspirations that may be filled
with clouds of falsehood for us. We are caught in webs of peer
perspectives with their tissue of class expectations. Intent on
being accepted in these quarters, we enhance the often shallow
ideologies and prejudices of the surrounding milieu. The ancient
Greeks spoke of truth as un-hiddenness, as a peeling away of
layers of illusion to reveal the true form of things. Such disclosure of reality or truth demands an arduous journey that must
always begin with ourselves. Midlife and elderhood offer us
better maps and equipment for this journey as an intentionally
planned trip. Inner and outer falsehoods become a depressing
burden by these later seasons of life. We know that time is short
and much is at stake on the pilgrimage to find ourselves as truthful individuals. We know, too, that the survival and health of
the world depends as never before on enough people walking
away from the falsehoods that will destroy the planet. The search
for truth today constitutes a dedication to the future life of the
world and its civilizations.

What does it mean to be honest about oneself? It signifies in
part an ability and willingness to question our self-understanding with its particular set of values. How much am I merely
playacting certain roles that have been mainly imposed by
others? I may enjoy my public images, but are they masks that
only cover up my true self-expression in order to fit into the
expectations of others? Or are these useful masks sounding
boards for voicing a true dimension of myself in the best sense
of using masks in classic Greek plays? One of the saddest aspects of retirement for some people is the general collapse of
their self-understanding (and esteem) apart from identification
with a job role. Yet the frequent occurrence of this retirement
syndrome should warn us against easy solutions about being

honest with oneself. Years of total immersion in a particular function can produce an identity fusion that makes rational reflection and will power incapable of fostering a change of self-image.

We must traverse another path by way of unconscious motivations that impelled us to choose such role identifications and cling to them so desperately. Whom are we trying to please? What goals are we pursuing in these roles? What hidden fears and doubts keep us from uncaging other birds of promise in our personality? When certain illnesses crop up in our mature years, it is valuable to reflect on them as symptoms of physical rebellion against years of psychic incarceration in unsuitable social roles. This is, of course, a tricky business, as we do not want to make people feel blameworthy because they have become sick. Surely organic distress has many causes. But the psychic component of physical breakdown has become important enough in our minds today to merit attention as a clue to exploring how truthful we are with our deepest needs. Since this road is hard to walk alone, the help of a spiritual or psychological guide may be imperative, especially for those who have had little experience with deeper self-scrutiny.

Uncovering layers of self-delusion in the quest for personal truthfulness relates closely with honesty toward and from others. To speak and act truthfully toward others presents a delicate task in responsibility. Here responsibility in its root sense means a discerning ability to respond in ways that honor one's own conscience and yet foster creativity in the recipient of honest talk. No little sensitivity is required lest we merely vent our spleens, saying things that poison relationships. A precondition for communicating honestly with another is a sense of the tentativeness or possibility of error in one's own estimate of the other. Are we judging impulsively or merely projecting our negativities onto others? The first step in honest talk, therefore, calls for a dose of humility about one's own judgments. Desiring the genuine good of another comprises a further criterion for saying things that may be hard to bear yet beneficial. Simply because something is true as an event of personal or family history does not mean that it must be expressed in any circumstance. The Christian scriptures speak to this point: The courageous, prudent person cultivates salutary knowledge. In this sense prudence signifies that delicate judgment of discerning between the cowardice of suppressing needed expression and genuine courage to risk speaking or writing truth that needs to be heard. One of the marks of aging with wisdom is the ability to exercise such prudence in the pursuit of truth.

How do we hear the truth spoken to us? Receptivity to honest expressions may also be complex and difficult. Its complexity arises from the possibility of multiple meanings being communicated in one form of language. For example, when a wife honestly expresses her thoughts and feelings to her mate, she may accurately reflect at least two types of meaning. She may be giving an accurate account of how she feels about a disputed topic; at the same time she could be making a judgment about the issue itself and her husband's relationship to the subject. Although these three issues overlap, they are quite distinct. As the recipient of such "straight talk," the husband may mistakenly blend all aspects of what was said into one overwhelming negative statement. He may hear her saying that (1) she feels badly about (2) an issue and about (3) his relationship to it.

In truth, she may be expressing only the first dimension, her feelings. Unless we can distinguish between such aspects of honest communication, we see ourselves under attack on all levels. As a result, we may respond with useless defensiveness or blot out the whole communication as too threatening. We fail to take in the truth spoken about the wife's feelings because it was not separated from unintended but clearly linked elements of the discussion. We need to cultivate the skill of first identifying what troubles us, and then asking for clarification in a nondefensive manner. As we grow older, we can become more open to speaking and receiving the truth, because we are more aware of limitations and failures in all human interaction. We shouldn't expect only rosy outcomes in matters as delicate and obtuse as interpersonal affairs. Because of this experience about life, persons in midlife and elderhood could be outstanding candidates for ever deeper truthfulness.

Still another dimension of truthfulness concerns our attitudes toward the world. Consider this on two levels. First, the lessons of nature can teach us a kind of honesty about ourselves. Nature reminds us of both limits and promise. The vision of the earth's evolutionary history tells us that we are only creatures of a brief life span. Each year the falling leaves and shortened days refresh our sense of the brevity of our time. In the realm of human potential and accomplishment, we tend to forget that our days are relatively numbered. Modern civilization with its artificial rhythms can easily blind us to the natural cadences of life. A part of ourselves wants to ignore the message of the passing seasons, the patterns of birth and death. Our technological era deludes us into believing that science has a remedy for all life's ills, even the final disease of mortality. Our mature years can become occasions for understanding anew the salutary lessons of nature. When we learn in an experiential way the truth of being temporary creatures, we can reassess our priorities. Given limited years, how will we choose to live them? Here nature does not discourage us but points to zones of promise. By deciding for more excellent priorities, we can leave richer gifts to our children. We can bestow on them a legacy of caring and sharing both in the personal sphere and in that of the ecosystem. Thus truth of nature is not merely a negative lesson about mortality and limits; it contains also positive truths about our responsibility, out of gratitude and wonder, for all the creatures of our planet.

A second aspect of truthfulness toward the world focuses on our political and social convictions. The aging person who remains enveloped in only private pursuits can hardly be considered psychologically mature. By "private pursuits" we mean an exclusively privatized concentration on individual pleasure and achievement. By contrast, the developing elder embraces a number of wider concerns from the welfare of his family to broader social causes. What does it entail to be truthful in these endeavors? It does not imply having the right solutions for political, ecological, or economic problems. Rather truthfulness requires a serious attempt to understand an issue within certain limits of time and of access to information. It further consists in a conscientious commitment to values that a person holds as his or her own, although these may be shared with others. This results in a willingness to take sides, to stand up for one's convictions and to act accordingly. On this level, there is no absolute, objective truth. But one manifests a genuine truthfulness of personal commitment and responsible action. Such truthfulness may change for an individual as circumstances and knowledge shift. But what stays the same, or rather develops, is the aging person's heartfelt commitment to social issues that can better human existence.

As you prepare for meditation with breathing exercises, repeat slowly the word "truthfulness" to yourself. Imagine layers of delusion and falsity peeling away, dissipating from around you. As your body shows increasing signs of aging, you desire to become a person of transparent honesty.

Starting with yourself, let the truth about your personal values move quietly before your mind. Are you honoring your deepest needs and desires or are you dishonest with yourself by embracing alien, conventional tenets and behavior? Perhaps you uncritically echo social, racial, and political views of your family and friends. Maybe you do things to seek the approval of others rather than act from your own convictions. As you relax more fully in contemplation, examples of such personal untruths will surface. Let these instances remain with you long enough to imprint themselves in your consciousness. You will seek ways to move away from such thinking and conduct.

You also want to speak the truth to others and receive it from them. Choose one, or at most two, individuals with whom you are most likely to have challenging encounters in honest communication. In the presence of such a person, see yourself speaking your mind kindly, appropriately, and with humility. Then turn the scene around; imagine the same person expressing feelings and thoughts about you. Notice how you may want to interrupt the other with defensive disclaimers. Yet you resist this and allow the other to finish. You try to clarify and understand his or her feelings and ideas. You allow the message to penetrate your defenses so that you can ponder it with empathy. You acknowledge that you have truly heard the other and will try to respond honestly when you can.

For learning truth from nature, look at whatever signs of natural birth, decline, development, change, and perishing that surround you. It may be the changing color of tree leaves or a sunset that ends a day, or possibly the aging of a pet you have known for many years. Whatever the point of imaginative focus, let the feelings of this event be strongly present. Nature will teach in a way significant for you its lessons of limitation and promise. The conventional dishonesty of your milieu will pale before the truths of nature. You are ready to empathize in truth with all other birthing, living, suffering, and dying creatures.

As a final moment of meditation, place before your mind an important social cause to which you feel especially committed. You understand that truthfulness in midlife and elderhood is deficient without fuller caring for others and expanding wider, universal concerns. You are becoming older with an evermore intense desire for authenticity in your personal life and in your responsibilities for the welfare of society and the ecosystem. You are becoming more truthful.

·11

DEVELOPING RESPECT

We speak about respect in two ways: being esteemed for one's accomplishments and as self-respect, the inner sense of personal worth. These inner and outer dimensions are closely intertwined, but they should also be reflected upon separately. From childhood onward, society urges us – especially in the middle class – to make something of ourselves, to do certain things in life that will merit the esteem of others. But the very actions that we acclaim and esteem in a production-oriented, technological culture are generally restricted to younger persons, who are judged to be more dynamic, creative, and adaptable. A few outstanding elders avoid such general categorization. But for the most part, the more we age, the less respect or dignity we will enjoy in the eyes of society at large. Persons who notice this trend in an acute way after retirement from the work world were probably undergoing a lessening of public esteem well before their retirement day. Again, exceptions to the statement might be those few individuals who hold economic and political power to the very moment of retirement. It is important to understand clearly the pattern at work in this matter. Social esteem, which for most people is the principal source of their self-worth, will gradually diminish as they pass fifty years of age. The descent will hasten if these aging individuals are also poor, less educated, or sick – mentally or physically.

The above may seem to be a harsh vision of aging in an ageist culture, but we must be willing to look at unpleasant reality. Not to do so only leads later to more profound disillusionment; moreover, to deny a pervasive culture pattern blocks our potential for growth along different avenues as we search for self-esteem. Yet to move from exterior to interior sources of worth presents an enormous challenge to most of us. It is easy to proclaim that we do not depend on others' opinions for our self-esteem. We may retort that since God loves us, this is enough. Or we may assert that our family of origin gave us such a strong quotient of love that society's attitude matters not a whit. But how genuine are such statements? Are they more likely propositions about how we would like things to be rather than affirmations concerning the true state of our self-assessment? Think back on an event where self-esteem was threatened. Perhaps it was the rejection of some project we had organized, or it may have been the failure to obtain a job or promotion. Public criticism of our work can have depressing effects. The list of possible threats to our self-respect from external sources can be endlessly multiplied. The point of this reflection is to underscore the difficulty of maintaining self-respect without a supporting community and some recognizable achievements. The truth is that we are all insecure about our personal worth. To acknowledge this fact can become the starting point for meditative modes to strengthen our inner sense of worth. As we grow older in an ageist society, much of our sustained energy for worthwhile involvements will be built on how firmly we have grounded the foundations of our inner self-worth.

Inner and outer sources of self-esteem, of personal dignity, work together in our lives. Parental figures communicated our earliest sentiments of confidence and self-regard. This is a very subtle type of communication that supersedes mere exhortations to think well of oneself. As children we indirectly absorb the nuances or overtones of parental inferiority feelings. We learn quickly how they see themselves vis-à-vis others in terms of social standings, educational level, occupational status, and the many other indicators of worth. Parental love, especially in its unconditional form, may have counterbalanced the negative aspects just mentioned. In spite of their own insecurities, parents may have instilled in us the fundamental experience of our worth in their eyes. If this happened to us, we had a fortunate start toward being able to increase our self-esteem; moreover, we were more likely to be trusting of others and to have a positive sense of what can be accomplished in the world. The latter will be a less-threatening place for us. Other relatives, friends, and teachers could have made special contributions to our self-respect by respecting us. They gave us the conviction that we had the talent to do something on our own and in our own way. Here we touch a corollary meaning of the word "respect": not to interfere with another, or more positively, to respect his or her autonomy. This fostering of a person's initiative and self-confidence by encouraging freely chosen activity forms a vital dimension of true respect. Such respect is the principal way to develop the self-love that gives one inner strength and a firm sense of identity. If a religious as well as psychological task in life is to produce men and women capable of loving, this network of respect-building becomes one's primary religious community. The grace of God operates in and through people of respect.

Inability to attain a reasonably strong sense of self-respect leads to many forms of destructive conduct. The shockingly high number of our fellow citizens who shorten or terminate their lives through ruinous habits testifies to a profound dearth of self-love or inner self-respect. Destructive addictions, for example, to alcohol, tobacco, and/or other drugs as well as to nutritionally poor diets account for a great number of unnecessary sicknesses and early mortalities. This is not to deny the importance of the more involuntary causes of illness and death: accidental, environmental, viral, or those produced by other external factors. But the psychological component of self-destructiveness rests firmly on lower self-esteem. At a very important unconscious level, people who continue to destroy themselves, when they may know better, are saying: "I'm really no good, but I hate the feelings of being worthless; therefore, I will continue to indulge in these harmful actions because they give me some measure of comfort or reprieve from my depreciating inner voices." Again, it would be simplistic to claim that lack of inner respect constitutes the only reason for such injurious conduct. Yet if persons deeply respected themselves, they would be much less prone to do things that clearly injure health.

Closely linked to physical well-being is emotional and mental health. Here again the overwhelming evidence from psychotherapy confirms that self-esteem or respect is a crucial element in healing the psyche. If we look toward the social realm, absence of respect plays a major role in all forms of violence. Various studies indicate that low self-esteem is connected with many types of criminal activities. Disrespect of whole groups of people for racial, ethnic, and political reasons continuously provokes outbursts of retaliatory violence throughout the world. On both the individual and social plane, a dynamic principle seems to be at work: When we are made to feel inferior and not worthy of respect, we tend to lash out with hostility. We witness this principle operating in interpersonal relationships and in the affairs of nations.

A different question concerns our ability to grow in self-respect. If the experiences of our early years deprived us of much inner esteem, can we make up for this deprivation in later life? Such a query opens a complex debate between different schools of thought. More pessimistic or sober experts would reason that childhood injuries to self-respect will hamper a person throughout life. We tend to agree, however, with those who offer more hope for growth in self-esteem given the right circumstances, even if one had poor beginnings. The "right circumstances" amount to the great blessing of finding a personal milieu of genuine care and love. We see no reason to maintain that such experiences in later years cannot mitigate earlier damage and teach people in an experiential way that they are respected and therefore worthy of respect. But just as this positive development can occur, it can also diminish and be reversed. For many of us the aging process through midlife and elderhood brings severe blows to self-respect. Simply being and looking older offends one's self-image in our youth-oriented environment. Physical limitations of actual disabilities increase with age;

these hardships become serious stumbling blocks to self-esteem for many. We may be shunted aside by younger persons in job tenure and advancement. If these problems are joined to poverty and illness in later years, the attack on self-respect can be very intense. Elderhood for such persons may become a long period of depression and even despair.

It is vitally important, therefore, to meditate on the roots, the foundations of our self-respect as we find ourselves in middle age or elderhood. We will want to review positive accomplishments in our lives. An immediate tendency will be to say that we have achieved little, but this means allowing ourselves to fall victim to the fallacy of great expectations. This error forces us to depreciate ourselves if we have not been awarded a Nobel Prize in some area, or written The Great Work or invented The Ultimate Machine. If we can temper the psychological inflation beneath such fallacious thinking, we will surely find many respect-producing deeds in our past. Some of these may fall into the realm of physical or material attainments for which we have some responsibility. Other actions could have been philanthropic or service-oriented. We may have taught younger people to think, evaluate, organize, administer, or build. In one way or another, we have probably helped someone feel better about himself or herself, thus fostering their self-esteem. As we review these events, the task will be to go beyond mere recognition of these happenings to experiencing – perhaps for the first time – the simple goodness of the event that has become part of our personal heritage. But an even more important method of appreciating our self-worth will be to recapture as experientially as possible memories of benevolence and unconditional love toward us. The point is to break through the hurried, taken-for-granted way in which we might approach such memories. We must learn to feel and savor the caring love that formed us and remains as unerasable a part of our psyche as our own DNA.

Prepare yourself carefully for a meditation on respect, because it is so vitally important to creative aging. Begin with the usual breathing exercises. After you feel relaxed and centered from quiet concentration on your breathing, you may want to introduce a mantra, perhaps "dignity" or "self-respect," into the rhythm of inhaling and exhaling.

During the first part of this contemplation, let the main demons of disrespect come before your imagination. Try to personify these inner spirits that tend to tear down your self-esteem. Even as we start this exercise, it should dawn on us that our major critics are not principally external, but rather inner forces to which we give excessive credence. These interior demons may have been partially formed by outside agents, but by midlife they are well-established residents of our psychic spaces. Which well-known inhabitant of your mind enters consciousness? Is it the inwardly appropriated figure of your mother or father giving expression to their own sense of unworthiness, sounds that you have made your own? Notice the style of these self-depreciations. Are the apparitions complaining about an unfortunate past, a bad marriage, squandered career opportunities? Perhaps they see themselves of no worth because of oppression from social forces: political, racial, ethnic, or religious? When you hear these old voices repeating familiar themes, you will be in the presence of the early sources of your own self-depreciation. Later personalities in your history probably reinforced these respect-lessening originators. The companion, teacher, spouse, or superior who in subsequent years added to the drumbeat of worthlessness was echoing the earlier lessons.

Choose one of the main characters. Discuss the matter with him or her from your new perspective. Now that you are older, you will be better able to understand how that person developed in a certain way and communicated an attitude of inferiority to you. Tell the figure that you understand this process, that you forgive him or her for the burdens unwittingly placed on you, but that now you must throw off the harmful weight of self-depreciation. It doesn't matter if the actual person is still alive; if you truly appreciate the inner configuration of that person as the real culprit, you will be able to distance yourself from the actual individual when he or she repeats the old ritual of self-depreciation. A crucial process of individuation is taking place in your adult life. You realize that you are no longer tied to nor incorporated into the collective mentalities of others. You are free from that bondage if you choose to be.

In the first part of this meditation, dismiss the old demon in a kindly but firm and explicit way. You might say something like: "I understand better the complex sources of my own interior mechanisms of self-depreciation. I am grateful for the many good aspects that you have brought into my life. But I must release you now as an esteem-destroying spirit that I have too long tolerated, even enjoyed in an unhealthy mode. Be gone; I must meet the challenge of my own maturity with greater self-respect. Not only my own growth depends on this, but also the positive gifts I will be able to communicate to others." Visualize the old image of depreciation slowly turning from you and disappearing into the distance. Savor the feeling of release, of a burden lifted, of a heavy door broken open to let you walk freely into the light.

In the final portion of this meditation, imagine another figure entering that open door. Let this be the image of a person who has been the most uplifting to your sense of self-esteem. He or she gestures to you to come out toward the newly lighted path. The figure restores for you in a tangible way memories of being appreciated as a worthwhile being. You realize, too, that this interiorized personage is now part of your deeper psyche. It is no longer the actual individual who in the past assisted your self-respect. For now you have incorporated this person into yourself. He or she has awakened your own archetypal source of the benevolent sage. Embrace this inner resource that will increasingly become your guide toward greater dignity and self-respect. As you understand your aging process, you too will become such a guide for others. In this sense, respect turning into self-respect is a self-perpetuating, upbuilding medicine for the soul. End the meditation with your chosen mantra joined to quiet, rhythmic breathing.

·12

RECONCILING OPPOSITES I

Midlife and elderhood offer the best opportunities for developing neglected or repressed aspects of ourselves. Given our limitations and insecurities during earlier years, plus the pressure of family and society to conform to certain expectations, we grow up one-sided or underdeveloped in areas that could contribute to our wholeness. Extreme examples underscore the point: talented athletes whose childhood and early youth were totally enveloped by a particular sport, such as tennis; or gifted dancers whose whole life from adolescence onward is consumed by ballet training. In similar ways, young people program themselves to achieve career goals with a narrow, driven perspective. The ideal of the Renaissance — a well-rounded education — is largely abandoned today amid the compulsions to specialize in technological society. While there are values to the discipline and dedication of such pursuits, we suffer great losses in fuller development toward an integrated personality. Much of our potential is wasted; moreover, we move into later maturity crippled and stymied by the burdens of one-sidedness. As the areas of overdevelopment lose their interest, we become bored and resigned to the all-too-prevalent existence of passive spectators.

This external one-sidedness relates closely to our intrapsychic imbalance. Jung spoke frequently about the suppression or neglect of human energies (archetypal forces) within the depths of our own psyche. To become more fully the person we were meant to be, that is, to develop our potential on all levels, we must attend to the reconciliation of opposites within ourselves. For example, various shadow dimensions of our personality tend to be covered over or projected out onto others, as individuals or groups. If we look closely at ourselves in group therapy, meditative journal reflection, or dream analysis, many shadow dimensions emerge. We experience a tension or polarity between opposing energies: our good and bad (as we perceive it) points, our acceptable and our inferior traits. The individuation process of reconciling opposites toward greater wholeness requires a new attitude concerning the dark or despised side of ourselves. We are to approach our shadow aspects as though they were rejected "subpersonalities" that wanted to give us special gifts for the good of the whole person. Instead of suppressing the clamor for attention of our shadow side, we enter into dialogue with it, owning it as a significant part of ourselves. In the language of Greek mythology, we must travel to Hades (within ourselves) to learn a type of wisdom that our daylight ego does not possess. The arduous journey into our own Infernos will eventually teach us about our full potential for growth. In a paradoxical way, we must confront the worst to appreciate the prospects for that which is better and deeper. If we live our whole lives with a one-sided view of ourselves as only children of light, we run the risk not only of a growing boredom and noncreativeness in our lives, but also of acting out indirectly, almost by reflex, the worst aspects of our shadow selves.

Still another dimension of our inner opposites flows from the contrasexual nature of being human. This means that men have inner feminine aspects, called the *anima,* and women experience masculine traits, referred to as the *animus.* Many forms of world literature – from ancient myths to modern novels – portray the tension between the contrasexual archetypes of *anima* and *animus.* Art and sculpture are also replete with this drama of masculine and feminine. We are born gender specific in the physical sense, but according to the concrete lessons of family and society, we also interiorize particular ways of thinking, feeling, and acting as boys or girls. In this formative process, the deeper archetypal energies of *anima* and *animus* are shaped in our personal unconscious into specific patterns before we are truly conscious of such molding. We learn appropriate manhood and womanhood in human society through the specific conditioning of parental figures and other cultural influences. We naturally and unreflectively internalize these images of masculinity and femininity. In myriad ways they influence how we think, judge, decide, and act. *Anima/animus* images reveal themselves in dream symbols as well as in waking life. What is referred to as a negative *anima* or *animus* gives us special clues to the particular imbalances in our personalities since youth.

The *anima*-possessed male easily becomes a victim of sentimentality and resentment. He withdraws into dark, sulky moods, ceasing to be objective or related to the world around him. Much of his conversation may express sarcasm or poisonous jabs. If an *anima* mood becomes chronic, it can lead to severe depression or addiction. His general attitude becomes: "It's futile; why go on?" A key to understanding possession by one's contrasexual side is the reflex or virtually unconscious way by which it dominates the personality. When we are "possessed" by something, we are so enveloped by it that we do not recognize its dominance over us. Reconciling ourselves with such an opposite, therefore, implies separating from it enough to recognize its runaway character. This means becoming newly aware of how imprisoned we men are by certain *anima* moods inherited from our earlier contacts with our mothers.

Thus the reconciliation of opposites, in the contrasexual realm, centers on the gradual process of curbing the negative *anima* and acknowledging and befriending positive *anima* images within. The positive *anima*, if attended to, can cure our one-sided sentimentality as well as our unnecessary machismo. When we as men enter into fruitful dialogue with our own archetypal feminine energies, we experience new capacities to be nurturing and empathetic. We can be led to a deeper creativity and spirituality. The middle years of life are an especially good time to encounter and to be influenced by this neglected inner feminine. Our self-identity in midlife is usually strong enough to allow us to appreciate the shallowness and perhaps the suffering of one-sided maleness. We are in a better position to see how we may have continually projected outward our *anima* onto certain women, imposing certain burdens on them and depriving ourselves of our own inner, nurturing resources.

A similar situation frequently exists for women who neglect the *animus* or who are possessed by it. The *animus* in its negative form endows a woman with rigid, unreflective opinions and convictions. She covers over deep insecurity with bluntly spoken dogmatic views that are nothing more than the conventional mentality to which she flees for some measure of self-assurance. She may sound outwardly harsh and excessively critical; actually the abrasive voice is that of *animus*-possession whose inner, accusing judgment erodes any true sense of her own value. When the *animus* forces unconsciously possess a woman, she is no longer able to feel and think for herself. No logic can shake the hardened exterior of banal statements and sweeping judgments. The encounter of men and women in the thrall of their contrasexual archetypes can be very destructive of relationships. The *animus* draws his sword of power and the *anima* ejects her poison of animosity; relationships wither. These negative entanglements cause such far-reaching injury in human affairs that it becomes crucial in midlife to step back, as it were, and examine one's own defective interactions with the internal contrasexual opposite. With reflective insight and perhaps the help of a counselor, a woman can cultivate her positive animus. The latter contains vital archetypal resources to help a woman analyze situations correctly, appreciate her own qualities, love herself as intrinsically worthy, and choose actions with courage and steadfastness.

The process of individuation, of developing as fully as possible one's unique potentials, is a lifetime task. The reconciliation of opposites in oneself is never finished. Moreover, the ideal of individuation is not to reach some plateau where the polarity of opposites disappears. The tension itself fosters creativity; ideally, we can grow toward greater wisdom and love to the end of our lives. We have reflected on two major sets of opposites in our psyche: the conscious ego and its shadow, the *anima* and the *animus*. It is important to realize we are dealing with conscious and unconscious dimensions of the psyche. It follows that we cannot force our unconscious "other side" to reveal itself to us by rational calculations. The archetypal aspects of shadow and *anima/us* possess a certain autonomy of their own. We must learn to approach them respectfully, in a meditative, listening mode. In such a receptive posture, we show ourselves disposed to learn the inner secrets of our soul.

To encounter unconscious, neglected aspects of yourself while in a waking state, it is all the more important to take time for settling into a deeper meditative mode. Take a few minutes of slow, deep breathing exercises with closed eyes. As you focus on this deliberate inhaling and exhaling, let the breathing process itself be a wordless invitation for your less-conscious "subpersonalities" to disclose themselves to you. If you are able to move into a state of self-hypnosis, dwell on your breathing as your spirit (breath as *pneuma* or holy spirit) calling to your hidden inner spirits. You are not approaching them out of idle curiosity, but rather to integrate better their insights into your whole personality.

When you have calmed and centered yourself in meditation, let two questions float about in your awareness, as if they were magnets seeking hidden metal. What qualities in yourself do you dislike and cover over as much as possible? What qualities do you most despise in other people? The first question seeks to bring to light the dark side of your personality, those potential behaviors that society and family have labeled as evil or those facets of you that elicit shame and are subsequently suppressed. Perhaps secret but forbidden desires will come to the fore. These may have to do with sex, money, power, or even violence. Such fantasies can be instructive for you in two ways. First, they help you recognize and own your shadow dimensions. They cure you of the notion that all destructive tendencies exist outside of you. In brief, these shadow images affirm the full scope of our humanness, our oneness with the inclinations of humankind. We can drop the illusions of a false purity of heart that frequently links itself to inflation of ego. But stay with these images long enough to experience how they are imbedded in your very being. When they are understood as part of your psychological makeup, you will less likely act out these tendencies than if you were oblivious to their presence in your psyche. For now you have some conscious choice concerning your shadow impulses. Return to the rhythm of your breathing; as you inhale and exhale, let each movement of breathing say yes to the presence of your shadow side.

Secondly, your shadow aspect can become a source of untapped energies for your life. By avoiding dialogue with your shadow, you diminish your potential for creativity. The very shadow images mentioned above — sex, money, power, and violence — have special gifts to give you if you know how to receive them. Hidden in these four words are neglected prospects for affection, value, ability, and assertion. Dwell on images that arise from your own shadow side as these pass across the screen of your imagination. Ask each of them to give you its hidden resource. You acknowledge that your ego is one-sided, partial, less adequate because it has not incorporated the buried strength of its shadow. Like a shaman, you are in meditation on a psychic journey to a dark and distant shore. In the Western imagination, this travel has been described as a trip to the underworld, to the lower regions, fearsome places but also zones of new wisdom and creativity. Picture yourself in the Hades or the Inferno of your shadow side; dispose yourself to learn that truth about you, a hard but enriching lesson.

Now shift your attention to contrasexual images of *anima* or *animus* as these may have revealed themselves to you in dream symbols or in waking life. If you are a man, you may wish to begin with images of your mother and other women that have been significant to you. If you are female, imagine your father and other men who have most influenced you. How have you taken these images within yourself? Perhaps their good qualities remain only outside of your soul, in these persons themselves, rather than incorporated into your inner psychic community. If this be true, imagine yourself taking each of these persons by the hand and drawing them into your soul to become inner confidants and sources of wisdom. You respect them as they were, or are, as individuals separate from you. But you also understand that they reside in your own unconscious realm, able to energize your life from within.

Conclude your meditation by slowly repeating your mantra in peaceful stillness. Let this personal and spiritual song, the mantra, heighten your awareness of your inner partners, who can assist your journey toward the reconciliation of opposites.

RECONCILING OPPOSITES II

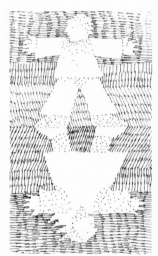

To grow toward wisdom and peace of soul in older age we need to learn from unattended voices within ourselves. When we hear these sounds with a renewed receptiveness, it becomes clear that costly battles are raging for dominance of our spirit. These conflicts are the clash of opposites, the often unconscious struggles of our ego to cope with threatening forces from our own depths. This meditation, therefore, continues the theme of reconciling opposites. In the previous contemplation, we pondered the archetypal images of shadow and *anima/animus*. Now we turn to other opposing dimensions of our psyche, aspects related to the interplay of archetypal energies but somewhat more recognizable to us in current psychological language. Many of us have gone decades without adverting directly to the inner clamor; we have drawn the blinds on it or tried to dampen it with various forms of personal or social insulation. We have so immured ourselves against the barking of the soul's hounds that we no longer hear their sounds. Such one-sidedness in life produces stagnation and increases fatigue within the unsatisfactory ruts into which we have fallen. Let us briefly open a few windows to hear the barking again in its full-throated urgency. Our inner dogs have vital messages.

Midlife offers an especially good season for facing the struggle between warring factions within our own psyche. By our middle years we may have grown tired of putting only more socially acceptable faces before the public, while denying other facets of our personality. We have looked upon these traits as inferior, as embarrassing, as cause for rejection. But many middle-aged individuals stand ready to reassess these earlier judgments about themselves, suspecting the existence of veins of gold amid what was considered dross. More secure with our basic self-identity, we can risk an exploration of our own presumed inferiorities. It may well be that "salvation" or healing or greater wholeness awaits us in the hidden or discarded realm of our inferior functions.

Everyone's sense of inferiority will differ. We may have so thoroughly covered over these unacceptable zones that they are actually hard to unearth. We may need some prompting to discover aspects of ourselves that we classify as inferior. Start with an assessment of your physical appearance. Perhaps excessive weight causes feelings of self-depreciation; or we dislike our smile, our profile, our height or lack of it, our color or lack of hair. In some way or other most of us don't like the way our bodies look to others as we imagine their judgments about us. People spend much time and money trying to cure their self-perceived physical inferiorities through clothing, cosmetics, and even plastic surgery. Of course, a certain attention to appearance and fitness is both wise and enjoyable. But the billions spent on forever cosmetically fixing our faces or our frames bespeaks deep-rooted worries about our unworthiness in our own eyes. What is to be gained by meditating on these images of physical inferiority in ourselves? Perhaps a new and joyful awareness will emerge concerning our sense of physical adequacy as well as the beauty of our own idiosyncratic uniqueness. The opposite in this area is the rejected body, carefully disguised with clothes and cosmetics. How can we become reconciled with our own physical inferiorities for the gladdening of the whole person? How can we be reconciled with our bodies so that we stop wasting valuable time and energy in unrewarding pursuits?

We may perceive our minds as inferior in certain ways. Maybe we have not had educational opportunities or possibly we failed to profit from those when offered. It may be, however, that our sense of intellectual inferiority comes from messages, direct and indirect, stemming from childhood and youth. We were made to feel incompetent, unknowledgeable, unable to grapple with important issues. Later we might have further reinforced this early training in schools where we settled for the self-image of being a mediocre talent. We simply defined ourselves as not-too-smart so that we wouldn't disturb ourselves and the world around us by challenging or shattering a fixed self-image. Like the ancient Greeks we thought it unseemly and dangerous to protrude from the given cocoon of a C-student; we knew our place; the cocoon was warm, soft, and safe. Or, on the other end of the spectrum, we may have concealed fears of intellectual inferiority by striving intensely to imagine ourselves before others as very bright academic achievers. Parental approval and affection could have been measured out by such accomplishments. With a certain trepidation we could thus uphold among peers the picture of ourselves as a superior intellect. But underneath the posturing lurked a gnawing suspicion of our inflated adequacy. We sensed this especially in the presence of superior minds, or at least those we thought to be such. However they were orchestrated, we need to confront anew our feelings of intellectual inferiority. What might we learn from the encounter? We might be thus able to release the envies and fears that keep us from embracing and exercising the considerable talent that is ours. Moreover, we will find an unexperienced pleasure in meeting, perhaps for the first time, our own genuine intellectual orientations and imaginative resources.

By midlife we are more aware than ever of our emotional inadequacies. Whether toward our children, spouses, or special friends, we understand the seemingly impenetrable blocks to expressing positive emotions and receiving such expressions graciously. This may be especially true for men whose formation restricted their emotional expression. For them the warmer or softer emotions were judged as signs of weakness or irresponsibility. Many persons have so long neglected their emotional lives that they are almost surprised to learn the truth of their one-sidedness.

Yet the clash of opposites, cerebral existence over against emotional development, works in a pernicious and undetected way. By middle age, a simmering dissatisfaction with living mainly in one's head troubles the person who increasingly senses that something important is lacking. Moreover, the life of the mind itself experiences greater barrenness and apathy, having been starved by the dearth of enriching nutrition from the emotional side.

Closely related to emotional development is the realm of personal relationships. It happens often enough that a new awareness of emotional inadequacy results from dissatisfaction in marriage and other close friendships. In our younger years, the pressures of achieving job success and raising a family may make us forgetful of the emotional qualities necessary for building deeper relationships. We believe that interpersonal relations will take care of themselves, as it were, automatically. Many men leave the fostering of friendship and social life to women. Those who neglect the interpersonal dimension, with its component of wider emotional communication, may awaken in midlife or later to the realization that they have pursued distorted priorities. They see the futility and emptiness of career goals without a strong ambience of love and friendship. Sometimes a failed marriage or job disappointment will cause a person to understand the shallow inadequacies that may have persisted for many years in his interpersonal relations. This perception of undermining or even destroying friendships through neglect and emotional immaturity can be a traumatic event for an individual. He may feel anger at opportunities missed and a disillusioned sadness for investing his life in directions that now appear sterile. The clash of opposites at this point becomes that between internalized career goals and the cultivation of deeper human interrelationships. Of course, such a conflict is not inevitable; some people manage to combine personal and professional life in admirable ways. But in our culture, which intensely stresses occupational and material success, the area of friendship and love, of caring and sharing in close relationships, is often allowed to deteriorate and collapse.

The battle of opposites rages within all of us. For long stretches of our lives we suppress or distract ourselves from facing the conflicts. We are too busy building a successful appearance in the world to grapple with inner insecurities. Yet we know that deeper personal growth is stymied by the refusal to recognize the inward opposites. When we arrive at a time in life of less care about external form, we understand that we must confront the tensions to get through them. Our physical, intellectual, emotional, and interpersonal feelings of inadequacy block the path to greater personal wholeness.

Begin your meditation with deep breathing exercises. As you repeat the process of slowly inhaling and releasing your breath, focus on the excellence of your body. We take breathing for granted; it happens automatically and smoothly for most people. But it is also a marvelously intricate confluence of muscles, nerves, organs, and the blood system. This vital function of your existence is an actual miracle, an awesome evolutionary event. Yet this is only one aspect of your whole body. Think of the miracle of sight, of sensation, of motion, of hearing, of speaking. What you don't like about your physical appearance pales into insignificance before the multifaceted splendor of your living body. What we dislike about our looks usually derives from certain superficial styles and fads of culture. As we meditate on the basic goodness and worth of our bodies, we are also more independent of social conventions and slavish compulsions concerning appearance. Without intellectual effort, let your imagination drift easily from your feet to the top of your head. As you visualize your body in its parts and as a whole, admire and accept it as the awe-inspiring mystery that it is. For all these years it has been you, your faithful vehicle for being in the world. If you feel so inclined, say a word of gratitude and admiration to your physical self. If you do not speak the words of praise, at least feel such sentiments toward your body.

When you are ready, turn to your feelings of intellectual inferiority. Imagine yourself in a situation where you typically experience intellectual deficiency. From one standpoint, you do not need to compete with someone who may know more or may have achieved more. See yourself honoring this individual's talent and enjoying an occasion to learn from him or her. Now you are aware that you can be discerning and evaluate what is being said or done. You realize that your mind is excellent, capable of expanding to many new horizons. As you grow older, you are understanding better that your intellectual gifts, your knowledge in various fields, can be shared with others for their welfare. Envision yourself drawing from your own experience to teach another person. You will abandon the depressing feelings of intellectual inferiority, knowing that they arise from useless comparisons with others. You will redirect the wasted energy of such defeating feelings into positive outcomes as you use your mental gifts to learn and serve. Become reconciled to your own intellect.

By midlife you realize more keenly that certain emotions have been suppressed or rejected in your life. The costs of such one-sidedness have been heavy in terms of achieving human wholeness. Allow one or other of these forbidden sentiments to come to mind. Perhaps you have associated gentleness with weakness, or at the opposite pole, you may have been taught to suppress the useful energy in your own anger as dangerous or socially unacceptable. Find the emotional opposite that is most foreign to you. Imagine yourself expressing this sentiment without worrying about predetermined opinions or supposed results. As you picture yourself expressing gentleness in a given situation, you enter more fully into your potential to be a loving person. As you imagine yourself giving vent to a certain degree of anger, you feel your ability to stand strongly for convictions, to be courageous before a challenge. This meditative exercise allows us to engage imaginatively in role-play with emotions, building a healthier inner dialogue toward personal wholeness.

In a final moment of this contemplation, imagine yourself at the center of a wide circle with a smaller circle inscribed within yourself. Each circle consists of precious elements held in a dynamic, magnetic tension. As the many aspects of both circles relate as opposites, an evermore excellent mosaic of yourself-in-the-world is created. Focus with gratitude on this living and struggling creation. It is an artwork that can become more beautiful with age.

·14

DEEPENING FAITH

Aging is a call to greater faith and faithfulness. But we must be clear about the meaning of faith that, like love, is highly conditioned in us by particular cultural experiences. Just as love for most people implies romantic or passionate feelings, so faith becomes linked with certain religious beliefs. People speak loosely of Catholic, Protestant, and Jewish faiths. What they typically mean is certain theological beliefs, moral obligations, and ritual practices that pertain to the human relationship with the divine. Faith in this meditation may be related to these institutional modes, but in itself it is a deeper personal experience of trusting knowledge or awareness. Such faith becomes especially vital in midlife and elderhood, because during these mature phases of life we are confronted personally with great dilemmas of meaning regarding our own life and death. The faith of childhood cannot meet this challenge; the calculated rationality of youth also falls short. If we withdraw from conventional routines into the silent zones of self-reflection, we can hear the voices that call to faith.

Whence do these voices arise in our soul? A genetic answer may aid our understanding. The first school of faith, as experiential, trusting awareness, happens in childhood. Whatever the ups and downs of the period, we derive from our parents a basic attitude about the trustworthiness or untrustworthiness of the world. From our own limitations and insecurities, we realize our dependence on some type of benevolent wisdom and care. Before any formal reflection, we know that we have to trust forces beyond ourselves; in keeping with how trustworthy these major figures are, we become more or less capable of genuine faith. If our parents were very unpredictable in their benevolent help, we may have developed a calculating, opportunistic, seemingly obedient faith in order to survive. But such opportunistic faith has weak roots and tends to wither in the heat of life. If parental figures were excessively dominant over us, we may have learned a form of subservient faith, again a compliance to win needed affection and favors. But the faith learned from an authoritarian context breeds resentment; it is often rejected for some kind of autonomous rationality by which we later guide our paths. For persons variously injured during childhood faith development, the road toward a mature, sustaining faith, is made more difficult, though not impossible.

The time from adolescence to young adulthood rests strongly on independent rationality. Surely, we are continuously nurtured by relationships of trust through family, friends, and a spouse or intimate other. But youth generally enjoys a needed distance from its own finitude and mortality. We are making our own way, hammering out our own future with reliance on personal discernment, choice, and action. In a technological culture, we are all the more enthralled by pragmatic reason with its ability to control and predict events. We live by many forms of "secular" faith during these years. We trust the plane and the pilot that will be capable of getting us to a destination. We trust in some form of fairness or justice in corporate and civic life. Yet we attribute much of the secular faith to the excellence of our applied science or the balance of interests in society that will maintain a reasonably just order. For all the problems of youth, much of it (barring a war, sickness, or other calamity) is a time of myopic safety. Perhaps it is a blessing that the inner voices are stilled for a while as individuals gain a certain strength of selfhood. For they will need courage and self-possession in later years when the old voices become more audible, even clamorous.

In the third phase of middle and old age, the earlier questions about faith will be asked in new, challenging ways. The parental world with its support systems will have been long gone. The rational confidence of youth will dim before the growing impact of one's own mortal meaning. Midlife invites us toward a more profound form of faith. For it is during this period that we appreciate in a concrete, personal way the limitations and paradoxes of life. We come to know experientially that the preferred dreams of youth, which we believed to be under our control, evaporate in the new dawn of paradoxical realities. Suffering and disillusionment in private and public realms make us veterans of life's struggles. We may keep up the brave front of youth, but in our quiet moments we know that the old protective walls are cracking and crumbling. What kind of trusting awareness is appropriate now? Is there a benevolent presence in and beyond us that can help us create new meaning—not a total meaning certainly, but a partial meaning that can energize our venture into the great issues of existence? Some aspects of the basic trust of childhood will enter into this new faith. But parental images writ large as God will not uphold the serious quest. Nor will the neat and self-serving philosophies or ideologies of youth sustain us in the face of the paradoxical mysteries of existence. Our own house of cards will crumble and the world, with its private and social evils, will remain resistant to remedy.

The quiet voices of new faith can be heard only in the silence and solitude of our own hearts. External promptings may help, but ultimately we must open up to the mystery within as it takes shape in our own personal history. In part, this new trust and assurance can arise from dialogue with the forces of our own unconscious. This repressed or neglected "other side" of ourselves will speak painful but necessary truths about who we are. It will also lead us toward a more complex yet strangely simple vision of reality and toward a healing trust in the living mystery around us. The new faith for aging will at the same time make use of the crumbling walls of our youth, cracking open gaps in our self-armature to make us more porous to the needs and hopes of other persons. We will be less judgmental of others and more attuned to their true spirit as it moves through the cracks of our defenses to embrace our own spirit. Through the new faith we will not have all the answers, but we will be inspired to ask the right questions; and we will be given the energy to walk toward the light and serve the world. The last point about service is crucial to faith for life's maturity. The new faith will be outward as well as inward. We will discover life's sustaining trust in the very work of social justice, human rights, ecological care, and many other forms of love for the planet. The new faith will neither still our doubts nor assuage all our sufferings, but it will make them supportable, even catalytic, as we experience greater human universality.

As we become more transparent to ourselves and universal in our sentiments and concerns, we will experience a new faith in God. We may balk at using the word "God" because of negative experiences with this concept in our lives. Moreover, this new discovery of the divine is not a rallying summons to adhere to this or that religious institution. Some will find traditional spiritual communities that enhance the process, but others may be empowered by seemingly secular encounters. What counts is the gradual acceptance of an ultimately benevolent presence in our psychic depths and in the outer world. This God, whether named or not, will at times be distant and disappointing. God may not reveal the vision you want, nor may the divine possess a totally final perspective. This God of mature faith may not have the power to change all evil to good; so much for the omnipotent magician of childhood. What good is a limited God? Many answers can be given to this query, but let us stay with one only. The God that is glimpsed and experienced in mature faith needs no justifying rationale. Rather, we experience this divine presence as a sustaining, challenging benevolence, as a suffering fellow traveler, in Whitehead's language, in the very inward and outward dimensions of mature faith.

Faith in and with God in the above sense is not an abdication of our freedom and responsibility. Faith "with God," on the contrary, denotes the importance of our creative involvement with the energies of good in the world. A planet where peace, justice, and mutual respect have a chance calls for a listening, energetic faith in cooperation with divine benevolence at work in the world. Such faith rests on no panacea; it looks through the glass darkly. On an individual level, we do not know the shape of our existence after death; it may be enough that we have experienced some love and beauty in our time, that we have passed on a torch of hope to our children. On the social level, no ultimate assurances undergird the human project. We may destroy life as it has evolved to this point over billions of years. As far as this earth is concerned, the forces of evil may prevail. Faith with God doesn't mask dire possibilities, nor does it expect magical outcomes from divine intervention. Perhaps the interventionist God is but a remnant of childhood faith in parental authorities that save us in spite of ourselves. Traditionally religious people have resisted letting go of the concept of the victorious God.

Mature faith for creative aging is a faith against the odds. It denies older age as a second childhood, as a return to the easy confidence of an earlier period. The call to faithfulness invites us to look into the abyss, into the void. Glimpses into the faith of Jesus may presage such maturity; "Let this chalice pass," and "My god, why have you forsaken me?" The Church of the gospels may have too quickly imposed an Easter victory on these disquieting words of Jesus' faith. It is terribly hard to stand before the void without the assurances that we crave. To age with faithfulness, therefore, means openness to the inspiration of divine presence in our psychic depths, our interpersonal relations, our communion with nature and in assuming responsibility for a better society. Faith with God is a faith with risk. Nothing less will measure up to the truth of things.

As you prepare for this meditation through the breathing exercises, think of it as a twofold motion. The exhaling will be a letting-go of false or facile faith, and the inhaling will indicate a desire to incorporate a more mature faithfulness. Remember that aging toward spiritual maturity is a gradual process. None of us can enter its advanced stages by merely willing it or even by imagining it to be realized in us by a guided contemplation. The goal of this meditation is more modest. It invites you to envision in your own way the shape of your fidelity as you walk through midlife and elderhood.

What do you let go? Only as much as you can sustain at this season of life. Recall in imagination the earliest pillars of your ability to trust. Perhaps these were one or both parents; it may have been another individual or a meaningful series of events. Let these early agents of your faith appear before you. Be grateful that despite their shortcomings (and yours) they started you on the path to experiencing the wider mystery of existence. Thank each of them; express gratitude for events that introduced you to faithfulness. As you concentrate on breathing, draw back into yourself these early gifts of trusting and trustworthiness; bring them into yourself again in inhaled breath.

But you know that certain patterns of childhood faith, less conducive to spiritual growth, have stayed with you. These aspects remain in your soul by adherence or by rejection. You may still embrace uncritically the facile assurances of childhood faith. In moments of personal truth, you recognize a certain dishonesty here; you want the comfort of the childhood assurances, keeping them away from the threatening scrutiny of your adult existence. Or you may have just as easily spurned the road to a more adult faith in protest against the abuses of religious authority. Under the guise of freedom and autonomy, you have created a secular self cut off from the challenge of wider mystery. You know best where you stand along this spectrum from adherence to rejection. Single out those major impediments to faith development in yourself; expel them imaginatively as you breathe out.

Apply the same dual moments of breathing in and out to the dominant themes of your youth. Perhaps a rational and pragmatic focus virtually eliminated the spirit of faith in the wider mystery of existence. Freed from earlier encumbrances, you saw yourself in control of your destiny, establishing yourself in the realms of self-identity and intimacy. Picture yourself in these important phases of your own becoming. Surely, there was much of value to be retained from these years. Yet what were the themes guiding your life that blocked your entry into experience of deeper faith? Formulate one or other of these themes and let their controlling influence flow out of you as you exhale. After a few minutes of this exercise, turn to those moments in life that caused you to question the basis of your motivations and worldview. Center on one or two events that may have upset your calculations, your chosen mode of living. Although such events may be painful to remember, there is within them a crucial message for your life's journey. Formulate this then and draw it into yourself as you inhale. Imagine this message being carried throughout your being, preparing you for the deeper reaches of faith.

As you look toward the years of middle age and elderhood, you stand at a threshold of more authentic faith. It will be no easy road, no light task. You will need all possible resources of mind and heart to enter on the arduous journey of fidelity. It will mean living with paradox, coping with ambiguity, struggling with seemingly intractable evils, risking a walk over insecure terrain. Yet you are willing to set out on a journey of faith because your own life experiences – from that of earliest childhood trusting to the most recent catalytic events – incline you toward a wisdom that transcends your own endeavors yet makes them more significant. As you conclude this meditation, focus again on the regular rhythm of your breathing. But now imagine that your breathing process is not an isolated happening in the universe. You breathe with God in the world; you are sustained by a benevolent presence that strives to be faithful and calls you toward greater faithfulness to the quality of life around you.

·15

HOPING

We the old have no future. Whether explicitly stated or implicitly meant, this statement expresses conventional wisdom. Having a future relates to a certain, sizeable span of time. Since the elderly usually lack such a time period, it is customary to think of them without a future. Modern life further confirms this notion even for those in midlife. Professional athletes are "old" at 35; their futures are behind them, as pundits say. The technological age convinces itself that only the young can keep abreast of rapid change; with this mentality, business and professional persons fear a quickly closing future if they fail to advance up the success ladder in midlife. Young people worry desperately about the future; will they succeed according to prescribed social canons? They enter college already anxious about being able to make a good living; the future threatens even these youngsters. Finally, over all of us, as never before in history, hovers the nuclear destruction of all futures on the planet. If the future is in such jeopardy, how can we age with hope?

It is very important to ponder hope. The German Marxist philosopher Ernst Bloch defines humans not primarily as rational animals but as animals-who-hope. If we have nothing to look forward to, we wither and die. The literature on concentration camps emphasizes a similar theme; some form of hope, of meaningful future, could spell the difference between death and survival under the most degrading and brutal circumstances. Judaism and Christianity are quintessentially future-oriented, hope-based religious movements. However one interprets Jewish Messianism, the latter cries out for a future time when hope for justice and peace link all humans. Christianity, too, is rightly called an eschatological religion because it strives and hopes for the Kingdom to come. The Christian movement has historically cast its lot so dramatically with hope for the future that, from time to time, prophetic figures have had to join this future orientation to the needs of justice in the present, lest Christians become escapists into a world to come. The humanist current of the last three centuries, as an outcropping of the Enlightenment era, forms a kind of secular religion of hope. The humanist values of political democracy, personal liberties, and scientific progress all point toward future possibilities, toward a hoped-for situation among people.

This historical digression bears directly on our meditation; it helps us to understand how profoundly steeped we are in a consciousness that longs for a better future. Inasmuch as this is true, how devastating it must be for aging persons to become convinced that they have no future. It is not hard to imagine the mental/physical injuries that can settle on an aging person bereft of any future: depression, withdrawal, illnesses, the temptation to despair. It is important, therefore, in our meditation to search for countervailing aspects of a possible future for ourselves as aging persons.

As individuals in midlife and elderhood, our future hope rests in cultivating the quality of time left to us. This requires for most of us, influenced for years by an intensely materialistic, quantitative culture, a serious change of attitude. Such a transition of mind and heart is no easy task. From childhood we have learned to associate power and prestige with material wealth. Our identity and security may be intimately joined to quantitative dimensions of life. Yet one of those dimensions, time left to live, is finally beyond our determination. Moreover, all the other

material items on which we place such value depend on that un-
controllable factor of time span. All these things die for us at our
death. When we shift to qualitative thinking about the future,
accumulated things and wealth take a different place on our
priority list. We may be able to find pleasure from the thought of
leaving gifts to our children or to society. But a change occurs
here: It is not so much the material items themselves that stand
foremost, but rather the act of giving to others, a qualitative activity. It is worth mentioning here, without extensive discussion , the qualitative or ethical aspects of how much we should
be able to leave to our families over against our obligation to
serve social purposes with amassed wealth.

But let us focus more directly on the qualitative aspects of
our shortened time as older people. The Book of Wisdom sets
the theme:"For old age is not honored for length of time, nor
measured by number of years; but understanding is gray hair
for men, and a blameless life is ripe old age" (4:8,9). And in the
same chapter appears the verse: "Being perfected in a short
time, he fulfilled long years" (4:13). In these lines the author of
Wisdom emphasizes values, qualitative perspectives as indicators of honorable aging. To dispose ourselves for such a future
we need to cultivate the ethical and spiritual values of our past,
giving them prominence in our foreshortened future. These
values will differ from person to person, but their criteria will be
similar: human welfare and respect for all nature. Some will
accomplish this by little personal actions toward individuals;
others will find ways to build community and love the world
through public-group actions. As their time span of life shortens,
such aging persons will enjoy a rich future of dedication to helping individuals and promoting peace, justice, and environmental
sanity. The essential hopelessness of material pursuit will give
way to a great hopefulness for moral and spiritual growth.

Aging people have a future through their connectedness to
generations to come. In our highly individualistic culture we
have lost worthwhile aspects of belonging to extended families
or to tribal groups. We rarely place the welfare of a community
above our own personal survival. And yet we remain highly
interdependent creatures. From birth onward we depend on

others for physical, intellectual, and emotional support. Our children and others under our influence will carry forward in various ways what we have contributed to them. The Jewish tradition has maintained an especially strong sense of this living on in one's posterity. Such smaller traditions, desiring to preserve a special identity in the face of oppressive forces, cultivate more intensely the idea of peoplehood, of being remembered by future generations.

Although frequently lost in modern society, the basis for such interconnectedness springs from key doctrines in Christianity. This would be particularly true on the Catholic side with its sense of corporate body, of organic interdependence of communicants in sacramental life. The church is spoken of as the body of Christ. Much popular piety has obscured the corporate sense of salvation with an exaggerated stress on one's personal status before God. If we could find a deeper spirit of peace and contentment with having made a contribution to the whole community through which we will continue to live, we can also find a source of hope in our later years. We will, furthermore, be inclined in elderhood to exercise special interest in and care for the generations to come, as extensions of ourselves, as our hope.

For many religious believers, the elderly have a future in God. We do not know the form of this afterlife, whether it will resemble the personal consciousness we now have or whether we will be remembered by God and in that way preserved in the divine life. There is no rational/empirical proof of such a state after death. Yet we experience a conviction of faith, based on our spiritual experience of God in life. Of course, much that happens in the world strikes us as shocking, unplanned, premature, or the result of inexplicable chance. Yet we are attuned to an opposite experience of a God who has sustained us, who is faithful to us over many years and whose fidelity gives us hope for the future. We move toward this future with a certain trepidation of the unknown; but we also walk on in the trust that the God who nurtures our existence will be able to uphold it in some manner beyond the grave. Such hope in the future can bring peace to our years and shelter us from excessive fear of dying.

✳

Assume a quiet, relaxed posture for meditation. Do a set of breathing exercises. Then attempt to visualize yourself as an older person, whether in midlife or elderhood. You understand that as you walk calmly forward in life, the future is an ever-shortening period for you. You acknowledge some apprehension about this as the clouds around the road ahead may hide pain and loss. Yet as you walk forward, imagine yourself pushing aside the accoutrements of power, prestige, and wealth that offer illusory hope. You respect all these things, but you set them in an increasingly subordinate place. You are becoming a seeker of more valuable qualities in the remaining time. Seeking truth, showing kindness and respect, doing justice, expanding your network of care—these concerns become ever more important to you as years go on. Even if time is lessened, it is lived at a higher level of spiritual and ethical intensity.

Bring to mind persons who are closest to you: family, friends, or perhaps younger associates. Think about what each of these people needs most from you at the present time. As you inhale, go within and find these qualities in yourself that you can contribute to these concrete individuals. As you exhale, see yourself giving forth this gift from yourself to each person. Visualize them embracing your gift and making it part of themselves. Just as your own children carry physical traits of yours, these individuals will become your future, because you will live on in them beyond your own death. Change the focus to some group to which you have made valuable contributions. Imagine this social movement attaining some of its goals and creating still new purposes. The group may well outlive you, but it too is your own future, the realization of things hoped for. Take comfort and satisfaction in this corporate union; you will live on in it.

In the final section of this contemplation, see yourself looking down a lovely road in a thick forest. Around the turn ahead appears a vision of light; you are amazed but not frightened. As the light approaches, you notice a luminescent human figure with hands outstretched to you in greeting. Suddenly you realize that the apparition is the benevolent presence of the divine coming toward you as your future. You do not know what lies around the bend in the road, but the vision has touched experiences in your soul, experiences that you have encountered before. You can trust the beckoning figure; it feels right to move forward into your future linked to God's future; you sense that around the turn in the road it will extend forever. You understand that you are part of God's future; your hope is attained; you are vitally at peace in the divine spirit.

·16

LOVING

To grow in one's ability to love through midlife and elderhood is a high ideal for creative aging. Yet the word "love," so frequently used among us, has many confused and distorted meanings. At times we say the phrase "I love you" in such a routine way that it carries little more significance than announcing the time of day. We talk about people falling in love; movies and media constantly bombard us with love affairs of one kind or another. We speak of loving our work, our cars, our pets, our country, our clothes, and our homes. The term is used so broadly that it risks loss of meaning. Despite the trivialization of love, we know that it somehow represents the highest sentiment and conduct of which humans are capable. We say that love is stronger than death, that it sustains our finest undertakings, that it is the noblest form of interaction. Amid this forest of often conflicting accounts, how can we chart some wise paths? What would it mean for us to become more loving persons as we advance in years? The following reflections* attempt to clear a trail toward a realistic and rewarding meditation on aging and love.

*In some of these reflections, I am indebted to M. Scott Peck's treatment of love in *The Road Less Traveled* (New York: Simon and Schuster, 1978).

Let us look first at love and the human life span. The key focus here consists in observing a gradual progression from narcisscism (centering on self) toward altruism (centering on others). Of course, the two poles blend to some degree at any stage; that is as it should be. For we can't healthily love another unless we also love ourselves. But the spectrum of development moves from self-pleasuring in infancy to some form of wider embracing of the world in older age, at least according to the ideals of these meditations. Love is the physical, psychological energy that, in more or less narcissistic or altruistic ways, impels us toward relationship or communion with the world. Thomas Aquinas held that the lover desires union with the beloved (object); in our psychological era, we should add that the union could be with our internalized "object" as well as with external reality. Although some individuals, because of mental traumas, cannot risk the union-seeking of love energy, most sentient beings long for completion through relationships with others. This observation is important because it underscores our profound sense of insecurity and incompleteness in ourselves alone. The same experience of lacking, of dearth, of absence lies at the root of both positive and negative forms of love.

Within this broad panorama of love as a universal energy, it is on the human scene more a matter of choosing than of feeling. It is hard for us to be convinced that love flows more from will than from emotion, although the latter is involved. This attitude among us results in part from the intensity of passionate love for another, and in part from the overwhelming cultural portrayal of sexual love. The impact of socially advertised romantic love becomes so great that people continue to crave it as *the* type of supreme fulfillment. They feel seriously disillusioned, cheated, and depressed when it eludes them. However helpful romantic love may be in uniting persons for a short time, it tends to be excessively narcissistic and it erroneously fuses separate identities. It resembles infatuation more than authentic love. Instead of allowing the independence of two individuating persons, such infatuation tries again and again to break down needed separateness by subordinating oneself to the beloved or by demanding that the other conform to one's own projected needs.

When emotion, based on a sense of insecurity and lack, dominates will, the genuine altruistic thrust of love is blocked. Instead of the desired union on all levels, persons experience the losing struggle of competing, misdirected emotion. Frequently enough midlife witnesses an apex of this battle for romantic love, as men and women enter into a final pursuit of distorted cultural dreams. Never having understood the true meaning of love, such persons may face an elderhood of chasing substitute narcissistic gratifications; they are blinded to the potentials of expanding altruistic love.

From what has been said, we can derive a working concept of love for creative aging: It desires, strives for, and finds personal growth in the development of others as individuals and communities. This does not mean masochistic self-sacrifice for others, which becomes merely another way of controlling others for narcissistic reasons. No, the healthy lover enjoys and finds personal expression in fostering the welfare of others. The chief point of difference between these easily confused forms of love resides in respect for independence. The self-victimizing lover ultimately exercises a dependency which controls others, whereas the authentic lover honors his or her own independent personhood, with its particular needs, and honors the separate personality component of other individuals. The Latins called it the love of benevolence: wanting the good of the other and growing/ delighting in the very process of the relationship. In true love there is something splendidly reciprocal going on: Giving and receiving happen at once for both parties.

But this type of excellent loving requires hard work. We resist the association of love with labor. We are led to believe that it is all a matter of chemistry, of spontaneous magic, of automatic feelings. Of course, there should be play and serendipity in love relations; the work of love is not drudgery. Yet by our middle years we know from experience that the "good magic" grows out of decisions and actions based on will, not on an amorous glow. Briefly consider the labor of love under five gerundive headings: listening, "othering," confronting, committing, and serving together. The gerundive form denotes a dynamic process in which all five aspects overlap, interrelate, and continually challenge us.

Love requires listening. We hear sounds with more or less attention during waking hours, but this phenomenon is mostly passive. To listen to another actively and well constitutes a high art. Through repeated bungling in this realm, most of us (especially males) by midlife recognize that we do not know how to be quality listeners. We think we are listening when we decipher words and concepts. We may be very quick to respond with well-intentioned, problem-solving answers. Yet in many instances we have not heard the real question or statement, which will have more to do with the speaker's feeling context than with rational solutions. It is easier to solve intellectual problems, because they usually do not threaten us personally. Yet there can be a wonderful outcome to listening from the heart, even when it may hurt. We may think that we contributed nothing but empathy; no brilliant solutions. Yet empathetic listening can allow a healing process within the other to progress. None of our incantations can produce this magic; a grace flowers from within.

Love calls for "othering." This manufactured word telescopes the idea of respecting the independent and different personhood of the other. This may be the hardest lesson to learn. Out of our own unreflected craving for self-gratification in a seemingly secure environment, we project our apparent needs or wants onto the other as demands. We refuse to permit the other to be a distinctively different individual with his or her own cluster of native qualities and expressions. This frequently results in stagnation, even paralysis in a relationship. Resentment builds and poisons interactions with indirect, displaced, or exaggerated anger. We suppress the authentic other out of our own ego insecurities; we are exercising a false power that seems to enhance us but actually hampers growth. Midlife conversions from dominant ego power to enabling power can open us to new ways of accepting the otherness of those we love. Only when we feel free to be who we were meant to be can genuine loving flourish.

Love means confronting. It would be both simplistic and harmful to expect "othering" to happen without the encounter of differences between people. Such confrontation is absolutely necessary for the development of a love relationship. Without it, one party, perhaps out of a mistaken notion of "othering," would have to repress his or her own feelings and ideas in conflictual situations. Life is full of events that lead to conflict and require a fair compromise. Here we are dealing with the essential negotiating skills or the diplomacy of love. As we know from experience, confronting can become a minefield of explosive hurts, anger, and accusations. Confronting is not the only way to exercise care toward self and other in a relationship. It may be wiser to influence events in less dramatic ways through suggestion, example, questioning, or creating new circumstances. But some confronting is inevitable in any close and long-term friendship. It is vital that lovers examine their own assumptions and motives before confronting each other; moreover, certainty about being right must give way to a more tentative confidence in one's own position. The art of confronting will often become crucial for deeper love relations in midlife and elderhood. It can allow spouses and friends to break through psychic blocks to new levels of mutual appreciation; it can permit children to have deeper relationships with parents.

Love entails committing. No relationship can grow deeper if the parties are half-hearted about investing themselves in its demands. Moreover, the commitment of love needs to be remade everyday, not only on solemn occasions like weddings and anniversaries. Two extremes surround the zone of creative commitment. One is the neurotic fear of commitment that plagues many young people today when they envisage the breakdown of marriage with its attendant hurts. This expanding population also tends to place career and material priorities above personal relationships. At the other extreme are those who stay in stagnant and destructive relationships without struggling toward new possibilities. Psychotherapy may help to heal some relational problems or to end destructive relationships. This plea for commitment wants to avoid both extremes. Committing allies closely with the benevolence of loving. Love means willing the total human welfare of the other(s) (and finding one's own growth in the process). Without true commitment, love turns into evanescent wishing. To commit is to make the intention of love real in actions. It calls for entering concretely into the sadness and joy, the peril and promise of loving. Commitment expresses the labor of love, whether related to adults or children. To love is to craft, to make, and to remake; it takes energy to build mental, emotional, and spiritual bridges across the gaps that separate us. The quality of our lives in middle and later years will depend greatly on our commitment to work at loving relationships.

Yet to become older lovers in depth also signifies reaching ever more toward unconditional loving and toward the wider love of serving the world together. With our closest friends and intimates, unconditional altruism characterizes the highest ideal of the aging person. Of course, the motives of our actions are always a mixture of self-interest and altruism, but a gradual purifying of intentions is possible. We may more truly advance toward this stage of altruistic loving after we have experienced in midlife the personal conversions from ego-centeredness to the letting-go of faith. We then understand our real vocation to enhance other lives and the welfare of the world. Therefore, as we age in close friendships, our interpersonal loving turns us outward together to embrace humankind in the wider natural world. Anne Lindbergh described such couples in the image of two seashells no longer facing each other, but rather linked together facing outward toward the world.

As we begin to meditate on loving, remember that ideals can be debilitating as well as energizing. Ideal aspects of love can discourage us when we reflect on how far our real relationships depart from them. Yet as aging persons, we should understand more easily the inadequacies of all human friendship. We want to approach this meditation with hope for small gains, with insights and feelings that will inspire positive decisions and actions. Realize that we are approaching one of the great mysteries of life, the art of loving. Some failures on the path are almost inevitable. We take little steps; we reach out tentatively with hope.

After centering yourself through breathing exercises, imagine that you are walking into a beautiful garden. It is in the form of a square with enclosing stone walls and a covered path along the walls. In the center of the garden stands a large, round fountain with water gently lapping over its circular tiers. The sun shines; you are alone with only the sound of water falling and an occasional rustling of leaves. As you walk slowly around the square, you are becoming aware that the whole garden contains the mystery of love; you perceive, too, that this is your unique garden, an outward image of an interior landscape design in your soul.

You desire that this place yield up its secrets, but you also know the revelations of growth cannot be forced. As you move about, you will allow key words from the preceding reflection to come back to mind: listening, "othering," confronting, committing, serving. There is no need to consider all of these; one or other word will speak directly to your needs. When this happens for you, sit on a rock or on a wooden bench and repeat that particular word as a mantra while you focus on the beauty of a tree or flower or delicate moss. Give the mantra enough time; don't hurry. Receive from the garden whatever gift rises into consciousness. It will have to apply to your concrete situation, to the network of relationships that is your life. Continue this inward/outward walk as long as seems comfortable. Accept with joy, conviction, and gratitude whatever blessings occur. You understand that you can always return to this special, enclosed garden to learn more about the mysterious task of loving.

·17

FORGIVING

Some statements from the past seem to stay in one's memory for years. I recall Reinhold Niebuhr saying over twenty years ago in a seminar: "Without forgiveness marriage would be impossible." This sentence brings together a great deal of wisdom not only about marriage, but also about worthwhile relationships for individuals and groups. Moreover, it lifts up a key topic for aging toward greater wholeness. All of us carry injuries to our personhood, inflicted by individuals and environments of our past. Sometimes these hurts circulate close to the surface of consciousness; when our attention rests on them, we experience a variety of feelings such as anger, resentment, and sadness. Just as often the injuries float freely in the submerged zone of our unconscious mind. These wounds are much more difficult to pinpoint; they impinge on us indirectly, causing feelings of depression or outbursts of anger that surprise us in their intensity. Some of these psychic wounds were quite real and perhaps larger in their influence on us than we appreciate. We may have inflicted other hurts on ourselves; but these, too, can dam up the sources of growth in the aging process.

Persons who do not deal directly with being forgiven for their harmful ways toward others or with learning to forgive run a great risk of becoming superficial in their mature years. A closure of inner psychic and interpersonal developments results. It is as though a valve snaps shut when forgiving or being forgiven wells up with memories of past hurts. The flow of energy inward and outward ceases; in this personality stasis, people divert themselves with trivia, even becoming bored with the surface sameness of their own blocked energy system. Yet it is very difficult to unlock the stream of our recollections and experience against the pain of childhood or later hurts. Persons may very well need the support of a knowledgeable and trusted guide to engage in such a process.

Let us also be aware in this exercise that forgiveness does not justify tragic actions and their consequences. If a child was sexually abused by parental figures, for example, later forgiveness of perpetrators may be fully consonant with condemnation of such deeds. The wife who may have been physically beaten by her husband or betrayed by him in other ways can come to a state of forgiveness without justifying such conduct. The examples could be multiplied on other levels such as public dishonesty, denial of human rights, or venal neglect of social responsibility. Most often we may have been hurt by less blatant and yet more complex, injurious conduct. It may be necessary to sift more carefully through our own participation in mutually harmful interactions. With these provisos in mind, we can explore four interlinked areas of our subject: being forgiven, forgiving oneself, forgiving others, and social forgiveness.

To allow oneself to accept forgiveness implies an acknowledgment of wrongdoing. The latter may be small or great, but the pattern is similar in all cases. We recognize our injurious action or intent; this requires a certain honesty and humility. In traditional religious terms, we understand ourselves as sinners, that is, we grasp the brokenness of our finite creaturehood. Of course, this moment of repentance can lead to excessive guilt, sadness, and self-deprecation. Such is not the true purpose of being repentant. On the contrary, this phase of repentance becomes the first necessary step toward reconciliation with others and toward a consequent uplifting of the self. Not only does being forgiven make us less inflated and thus more authentic, but it also re-stores our communal bonds; we are enriched by being embraced back into community. Being forgiven means letting ourselves experience our dependence on others for wholeness; we are not self-enclosed, self-sufficient beings. We must realize, however, that being forgiven does not consist in some kind of magical rite that instantly makes us feel better without having to undergo a serious resolve to alter our injurious ways. Without a conviction that we must learn to transform our harmful conduct, being forgiven degenerates into an insincere and farcical ritual. As we move into middle age, we should have less need for the self-inflation that blinds us to our faults. We have experienced our shortcomings long enough to want to transform them into something better. We are prime candidates for the reconciling influence of accepting forgiveness.

By the time we are middle-aged or older, we may have become our own worst enemies by developing patterns of self-denunciation. Many people seem incapable of exercising forgiveness toward themselves. They excoriate themselves for mistakes, accidents, or failures. It would be too complex for our purposes to trace the origins of self-victimization in a personality, but we should consider some aspects of this masochistic conduct and its unfortunate outcomes. We allow ourselves to become needlessly depressed and self-deprecating, taking a kind of unhealthy plea-sure in our own victimhood. Moreover, we tend to spread our self-polluted consciousness to those nearest us, especially in our own families. It becomes easy for us to draw these bystand-ers into our unforgiving circle as our persecutors. Full-blown self-victimizers can't seem to persecute themselves enough; they need to rally help in the endeavor. If these personality pat-terns continue into later years, they can lead to severe depres-sions when the disabilities of age add extra burdens. Such people become ever more centered on their aches and pains, losing con-tact with and interest in significant issues beyond themselves. It is vitally important to change such patterns, in part through learning to forgive oneself.

By midlife we not only know better our own failings, but we also understand more clearly the injuries suffered over the years.

Because we have lived longer, more hurting events – psychological, physical, and economic – could have befallen us. But even more important, our personal identities are usually secure enough by our middle years to permit us to assess with candor and balance how others may have hurt us. Let us recall again that forgiving another's offense doesn't necessarily mean justifying the action or returning into regular contact with the harming party. Yet the act of forgiving another may cause us to mitigate our rage and also place the hurtful event in a nuanced light. In the best circumstances, forgiveness fosters reconciliation between persons; the areas of estrangement are diminished. When we say "I forgive you" with sincerity, not as a ruse to dominate, we allow the other to be healed within. In forgiveness we also stem the malady in ourselves of gnawing grudges and poisoned sentiments. We embrace the brokenness of the world and acknowledge our own possible complicity in the wrongdoing. Therefore, in true forgiving a threefold dynamic manifests itself. The offender can find inner healing; we open our souls to the broken reality of things in our share of the breaking; and finally, we experience community at a deeper level. At times, forgiveness of another can join people into stronger ties of friendship. The point of forgiveness resembles the welded place where broken metal is rejoined. At the very juncture of the damage, the new weld becomes the strongest part of the whole repaired portion.

According to our ideal of the aging process, we are called to become reconcilers amid alienated human groups. As we advance toward an elderhood immersed in the great concerns of humanity, we must examine our hearts about rancor and hostility against groups that have hurt us. Examples of such communal alienations abound. From a racial perspective, blacks carry a history of injury in white societies; from ethnic-political vantage points, Arabs and Israelis point to continuing offenses of the other; in a religious optic, the Baha'is in Iran have suffered greatly as heretics in a Shiite culture. Forgiveness by itself will not right the wrong deriving from political-economical pressure, religious intolerance, and deep-seated historical enmities. But a spirit of forgiveness can curb the animosity in our own hearts toward the enemy group. This spirit keeps us from becoming mired in our stereotypes about the other group. We remain flexible and open to all gestures of reconciliation. Flexibility and openness are virtues said to be lacking in older persons; the opposite should be true if we have tried to develop a forgiving spirit from our middle years. Elders, in their own associations, are called to become catalysts for forgiveness toward alien groups.

Do a few breathing exercises as you prepare yourself for a contemplation on forgiveness. Remember that the purpose of these preliminary actions is to center your attention and calm your mind to be able to receive insights. When you feel sufficiently relaxed, draw into your imaginative vision a person whom you have wronged. Think about your own family or possibly occupational colleagues. Call to mind the nature of what you did, or perhaps what you do on a regular basis, that hurts the other. Sense the pain and disrespect involved. Explore your own heart for any feelings of sorrow and repentance for your actions. From this position of contrition, ask pardon of the offended individual. You then imagine this person forgiving you, and you accepting the forgiveness. Perhaps the two of you embrace or mark this reconciling moment with some other gesture. Stay with the feeling of being forgiven as a source of renewed energy to live in a more reconciled way in the future.

Choose a person who has injured you in a serious way. Let this individual stand before you in imagination. Recall again what you can of the hurting times when the offense was most acute. You are going to let the pain of this flow out of you with each breath exhaled; for it is futile to hold onto this hurting; you have suffered enough from it; let it go as it only impedes your growth as a maturing person. There is probably no way for you to change what happened. As you free yourself from the pent-up hurt, you will be more able to look with charity at the person who injured you. Whether the offense was mainly from weakness or from malice, you now understand from longer experience the burden of insecurity and other shortcomings from which people act. While you hope and strive for more gracious, caring human interactions, you no longer view the world with the untried and brittle idealism of youth. You have faced the ignorance and even meanness in yourself as sources of harming others. You forgive this person, wishing him or her well, desiring happiness and growth toward wholeness in them.

Imagine yourself in a typical session of self-blaming, if you are subject to such conduct. Reenact the self-accusations and let the negative feelings course through you. When you think that you have sufficiently rehearsed such a scene, be still for a few moments, attending to the rhythm of your breathing. Slowly place both hands palms down on your forehead. Imagine a forgiving, healing energy radiating through your hands down into the rest of your body. This laying-on of hands symbolizes an act of forgiving yourself. You are freeing yourself to go forward toward maturity without the cycles of self-recrimination. By unburdening yourself of these fruitless episodes, you are also becoming more kind to those around you; no longer will you have to let anger at yourself spill over onto others. You know that if you are to grow older as an agent of peace in the world, you need first to make peace within yourself.

Finally, select a group that you dislike, perhaps intensely. Position yourself among people who oppose the alienating group for whatever negative intentions and actions they demonstrate. It should be easy to recall the bad points of the other group. Examine also the type of feeling you have toward them. Is it mostly contempt, fear, pity, or revulsion? It is important to know how you really feel about these people if you are to move toward forgiveness. Now try to place yourself in the social and ideological milieu of a member of the other side. How has such a one experienced life, how would he/she perceive you and your group? Can you enter empathetically into a mentality that may be strongly threatened by what your group embraces? Through such understanding of your "enemy," you can gradually advance toward forgiveness and reconciliation.

If you are able to take a further step beyond simply understanding, say to these opponents, "I forgive you," "I will work among my own people to foster better understanding of your fears, wants, and needs." Insofar as you can do this, you are becoming an older person of reconciling forgiveness. You are becoming the forgiving mercy of God, because you have experienced the blessing of forgiveness in your own life.

·18

CULTIVATING JOY

Lacrimae rerum the Roman poet said about life: the tears of life, the sadness of reality. The aging person who seriously contemplates the world knows what the ancient bard meant. Tragedies and misfortunes abound; some happen as accidents of nature, others through human neglect, ignorance, and malice. A certain sadness comes over us when we empathize with these events. Feeling the sadness helps to mature and deepen our spirits. But these experiences can depress us when added to our own history of sorrows. In this realm we can sight the clearly traumatic occurrences, whether mainly physical or emotional and mental as well. Yet even beyond these memorable events in our lives, a more subtle or hidden agent of sadness often lurks.

Nietzsche referred to this as the spirit of gravity which oppresses the free expressions of the creative child within us. For a variety of reasons, we submitted ourselves early in life to certain scripts that still rule our thinking and behavior. Many of these injunctions, "thou shalts," imposed by family, religion, and culture have buried the vital "I am" of our lost child. So immersed are we in the spirit of gravity that we hardly even recognize it. Sometimes we sense the need to break old scripts and respond differently to the world. But joy escapes us. Even our successes do not bring the joy we anticipated. Midlife and elder-hood become prime periods for reassessing our victimization by sadness. What is the meaning of joy and what are steps toward it? Definitions of states like joyfulness always fall far short of the experience itself, but we may learn something useful by examining various traits of being joyful. Of course, these posi-tive aspects of joy admit of varying degrees of intensity; more-over, they come and go according to many circumstances of life.

The joyful person experiences a heightened sense of vitality. He or she can say that it feels good to be alive. It is less a matter of being made happy by some external happening, though such an event can enhance one's joy. Rather, joyful vitality stems mainly from an interior status of knowing and accepting one's own worthiness. To see oneself as worthy does not entail making a superficial judgment about one's value, as though no problems or deficiencies exist. Nor does respecting oneself as intrinsically worthwhile signify prideful inflation. The vitality of joyfulness consists in a less defensive and therefore more truthful and serene embracing of one's own inner value apart from the judg-ments of others. Occasionally we encounter an older person who exhibits such vitality. In the presence of such a one, we sense an almost indescribable quality of self-possession that radiates joy from within. This individual may suffer various disabilities and may have experienced considerable hardship in life. Yet the problems only heighten and surround a peaceful joy at the center of personal existence. The elder who can mirror such an attitude of joy from his or her depths becomes an inspiring personality for many who may not have known that such a way of living was possible.

Inner joyfulness, therefore, radiates outward in attitudes toward others and toward the world. People who meet a genu-inely joyful person feel a certain ease enveloping such an individ-ual, because they realize that no special performance on their part is needed to sustain his or her inner joy. Nor do they feel under judgment by this joyful individual; he or she doesn't need to judge others to find happiness in a kind of superiority by comparison. The joyful person is not in competition with them, as though elation could only be achieved by lifting oneself over others. Thus others are influenced by the joyful one less by what is said than by experiencing an unspoken acceptance of themselves for what they are. Nor is joyfulness incompatible with criticism of others, even anger expressed toward others. For both the anger and the criticism do not express a need to dominate or deprecate others. We know that the critique is meant for our good, to help us avoid destructive ways that will impair our ability to achieve inner joy.

The joyful elder manifests a positive attitude toward the world without denying its many problems. This stance toward reality implies the deeper sense of trust that we considered in the meditation on faith. Human stupidity and malevolence may indeed destroy life on this planet. The joyful person feels anger and sadness about that prospect, but he or she perceives the world as less threatening. Put another way, the paranoid individual feels virtually incapable of joyfulness; existence is too menacing at all times to permit such a relaxed attitude toward reality. The person who ages with such a mentality will not become a good counselor to younger generations. He or she will stimulate fear of enemies and the psychological projections that fuel such fearfulness. As we grow older, therefore, it becomes most important to cultivate the seeds of joyfulness within ourselves. For true joy, not mania or frivolity, is contagious. We exercise an uplifting social role by demonstrating joy to those we encounter.

Joy, whether quiet or intense, involves an experience of transcendence. We act not merely from a grudging motivation of deficiencies, that is, making up for what we don't have in the material, intellectual, or social spheres. Even when we are busy fulfilling our physical or psychological needs, joy adds a kind of surpassing dimension. We delight in the very ability to perform the ordinary tasks of life. Joy reflects transcendence, or a going-beyond, because it puts us in a state of "overdrive," as it were. We may be performing actions that we have done many times, but in a spirit of joyfulness these behaviors are suffused with an aura of gratitude, wonder, and pleasure. These qualities blend into the transcendent experience of joy. This transcendence of joy is not an escape from the present moment into wish-fulfill-ment aimed at the future. But joyfulness presents a heightened sense of what we are actually doing now.

Another way of expressing this aspect of joy relates to the vividness of our perception of ordinary things. All too frequently, we experience only a small fraction of our actions and of our environment. We are too preoccupied or driven by some external constraint to be able really to focus, to see vividly in the present moment. Joyful transcendence raises us above these compulsions to a clearer perception of the experienced present in its multifaceted qualities. In this way, joy also opens us up to novelty, to see creative possibilities in our situation. The transcendence of joy melds with creativity: New options appeared in what was thought to be a set of closed circumstances. In this breaking out of old scripts and into an adventure of novelty, joyfulness becomes an eminently religious experience. Religiousness in this context means the elevation of our perceptions and sentiments into a fuller network of possible future connections.

Humor is also related to joyfulness. Aging persons who cannot laugh at themselves and with others have missed life's powerful message of incongruities and surprises. The traumas and sorrows of existence must not be taken lightly; we suffer and mourn. Moreover, serious responsibilities press on us from many directions in our mature years. We cannot shrug off these concerns with a laugh. Yet for a joyful person the pain and responsibility of life are themselves enveloped in a broader context. A sense of humor permits us to bear and use our sufferings rather than to be simply victimized by them. Humor implies that we can observe ourselves from a certain distance and gain some perspective on what happens to us. Responsibilities can be carried more sanely when we realize how little we actually do for other individuals and how little actual control we have over them. If we are ready for irony and humorous surprise, we will assume our responsibility with a greater gentleness of spirit, expecting to laugh at our overseriousness. Without humor, deeper love may not be possible. For humor reminds us, through its surprises, of the distance, the otherness of the friend or spouse. We cannot comprehend and dominate the others; humor thus breeds respect.

In a similar way, humor may be vital for coming to know God. It teaches us to respect the inscrutable ways of divine providence, and in the style of Jewish tradition, humor allows for a kind of semiserious dialogue with God. Crucial here is the relationship between humor and keeping open to, staying free for, the possibility of novelty disclosure. Without this important dimension, religion can become nothing more than the projection of our own fears and of collective necessities onto some divine image. True humor subverts the lust for dominating power. Listen for the tone of dominating power in many serious sermons. The preacher will claim to have absolute answers to human dilemmas. One can almost feel the minister's need to assure himself and control the lives of others, justifying it all, of course, by reference to selected biblical passages. Humor helps cut open the net of overweening seriousness, itself a disguise for dominance.

As you begin to meditate on joy, doing the breathing exercises, reflect on its importance for aging well. By now in your life, you have experienced the *lacrimae rerum*. You have suffered and you have empathized with the sufferings and sorrows of others. These experiences are not the enemy of joy; rather they form the maturing ambience for a deeper joyfulness. The real adversary of joy is a life that hides the pain of existence beneath a veneer of superficial diversion and empty laughter. When you feel quiet and centered, you are ready to contemplate sources of joyfulness for yourself.

In the first moment of meditation, picture yourself still or in motion. The image that you see becomes transparent to your eyes, as if you could look with x-ray ability to see deep inside of yourself. Within this awareness, you approach the sources of your own vitality. Recall a time when you felt happy, not from some external event, but simply because you rejoiced in your own talents and inner qualities. Remember the quiet but strong joy in the depths of your soul. As you recapture that sentiment in memory, join it to the transparent image with which you started this moment of meditation. Stay focused on the vision and feeling of yourself as capable of generating joyfulness from within your own being.

When you are in touch with this inner joy, you can radiate joyfulness to others. Imagine yourself in a group of peers or of people who are under your charge. Notice that you can let go of competition and envy as you deal with these associates. Since your main joyfulness springs from within you, you have no need to dominate others or feel cheated if they win honors for their accomplishments. Rather your own joy becomes enhanced by participating in theirs. As you grow older, you understand ever more fully that the great problems of individuals and groups in the world need to be approached with the energy rising from joyfulness. The enormous issues of personal crises as well as those of hunger and war among nations can crush spirits, immobilize persons in sadness and useless negativism. As you advance toward elderhood, you realize as never before how essential it is to encounter problems from the indomitable power of your own joyfulness linked to the dynamic energies of others. Imagine light and warmth emerging from your transparent image fusing with the joyful energy of others. Imagine this positive force encircling the planet to sustain and enrich it.

The experience of joy will lead you to new dimensions of spirituality as you grow older. You will discover that the transcending experience of religiousness emanates chiefly from your own joyful depths. Transcendence means going beyond. As a joyful elder person you will be enabled to break through the prison of life scripts that may have hampered your development. Joyfulness allows you to transcend by perceiving the ordinary happenings of your existence with a new vividness. You begin to grasp your smaller world as a part of a larger mosaic of meaning. The transcendent experience of joyfulness raises you far enough above this mosaic of significance to be able to see the small pieces as part of a wider whole. There is adventure in this new interconnectedness; options will open up that had not been noticed before.

As you conclude the meditation, marvel at the ways by which joy can surprise you. Incongruity forms the heart of humor and laughter. If you have rediscovered some degree of inner joyfulness, you too will know that the experience is a more surprising gift, a grace, than anything you could ever give yourself by strenuous effort. If the experience of your own resources of joy brings a smile to your face, you are mature enough now to realize and humbly accept the ironic gift of your own joyfulness.

·19

OPENING TO CREATIVITY

 Can we age creatively? Most people do not associate creativity with older persons. We expect elders to approach their later years as a kind of prolonged vacation, a well-deserved rest after a life of work. This attitude toward the last third of life conjures up ease, even passivity, rather than creativity. The latter connotes a making, a shaping, a bringing of something new into being, and of existing oneself in an intensely productive way. A few elders remain creative to the very end of their lives; in almost every field outstanding individuals continue to make valuable contributions to society and to open up new avenues of growth for themselves. Yet so many settle back into conventional routines, staying in familiar ruts that dull their potential for creativity.

We are not confining creative existence to those exceptional thinkers, doers, and artists who achieve great fame for their creations. The combination of talent, skill, motivation, and a uniquely stimulating milieu that is the mixture for works of genius must surely be expected of relatively few. Yet if we restrict creativity to such extraordinary figures, we tend to minimize the creative potential of most people. Moreover, such narrowing of the concept allows us to excuse ourselves from the endeavor of tapping our own creativity as we age. Rather than discourage us, however, the aging genius can be a source of splendid inspiration for us. Aging geniuses show us that it is never too late for creative activity.

To be creative means enhancing our personal integration by pulling together in novel ways the disparate and conflicting strands of our existence. It also signifies efforts at fostering social integration of opposing forces in ever new ways. Individual and communal creativity are two moments of the conjunction of opposites by which we experience deeper awareness of the paradoxical union of self, other, and world. We will no doubt grow old according to the traits we have cultivated earlier in life. If we hope to be creative in elderhood, we need to cultivate the qualities of creativeness as early in life as possible. Although the traits of creativity should be fostered from one's earliest years, midlife lends itself particularly well to developing these dispositions.

A certain independence of mind marks the creative individual. By middle age we can be secure enough in our own identities to question and distance ourselves from cultural expectations and conventions. We realize that conformity to previous life scripts has hampered the development of our neglected potentials. Moreover, we see more clearly the failed promises of earlier career choices and life-styles. Yet for creativity to become actual in our lives, we must join this independence of spirit to ego strength and assertiveness in pursuing new directions. For we may be independent enough to see things as others do not, yet lack the courageous determination to choose and act according to our insights. In a paradoxical sense, ego strength also allows us to regress into our unconscious zones, into fantasy and contact with primary processes, knowing that we will be strong enough to return to our basic identities.

A second set of qualities of the creative person concerns receptiveness. In a certain way, this cluster of traits reveals a kind of passive perceptiveness. The creative individual lets conscious awareness and unconscious symbols or feelings enter into the mind without trying to impose an immediate, conventional ordering or judgment on the material. He or she is willing to look at and be affected by the whole unruly forest before attempting to name the trees. It is a matter of understanding and empathizing with a whole context rather than centering quickly on a particular item. This attitude demands a patience that takes years to learn. Such patience must not be confused with uncaring passivity; rather it is an intense activity coupled with a desire for discovery. It is at once an active immersion in the data and a detached devotion to the whole picture in its complexity. By midlife we should realize in an experienced way our ignorance about people and the world. Patience recognizes this dearth of understanding and gives reality a second or third chance, as it were, to transform our ignorance into what in the medieval era was called *docta ignorantia*, learned unknowing or ignorance. This creativity in any field calls for a blending of a strong independence of spirit to a patient sensitivity so that the lessons of life can instruct us.

A third grouping of traits for creativity focuses on a tolerance for ambiguity, complexity, even disorder. Out of our need for security, we tend to impose order on stubborn and threatening diversity. It is difficult for most people to hold competing ideas and movements in all their challenging complexity. Yet by the time we approach elderhood, if we haven't lived in a closed universe, we know experientially that reality is both complex and ambiguous. This is true not only in the intellectual realm of science and ideas, but also on the level of interpersonal and societal relations. If an elder is to become a creative peacemaker, for example, he or she must break through the fear of diversity and ambiguity in human affairs to discover the rewards of living a more complex life. The latter does not mean a life of haste and hyperactivity. On the contrary, a complex life, which may be lived in thoughtful serenity, entails letting the real world in its full diversity unfold on the stage of one's mind and imagination. This calls for an ability to hold and compare many ideas at once, moving to ever wider syntheses while respecting differences. It means welcoming a critical interplay of creeds, theories, and practices. The elder who develops this level of creativity in thinking, judging, and acting is in a better position to work as a peacemaker among contending individuals and groups. He or she learns to profit from past errors and to ask the right questions that lead to more satisfactory solutions.

These qualities of the creative elder, however, do not develop in a vacuum. Just as they must be fostered as early in life as possible, they also need a supportive social setting. If we think about great creative genius, the importance of cultural milieu becomes evident. Michelangelo, Newton, or Jefferson, while possessing extraordinary gifts as individuals, would never have attained their heights without the stimulation of special cultural, scientific, and political environments. Picasso and Chagall, Albert Schweitzer and Martin Luther King, Jr. would not have made their significant contributions outside of a particular formative, provocative, and yet sufficiently supportive milieu. For some, like Kierkegaard and Van Gogh, an ambience of hardship and even discrimination spurred on their creative efforts. A social context of interaction with significant persons engenders the creative potential of such figures. When we reflect on extraordinarily creative individuals, we also must resist the temptation to become discouraged by comparison. All of us have creative gifts to offer on many levels. Some will be able to foster new thought, action, and feeling in others on a quiet, one-to-one basis. Others will make special contributions in a more political or social context. The great geniuses of history prompt us to live our own potential to the fullest.

We learn from this communal aspect of creativity that it will be vital for us as aging persons to find stimulating environments. To achieve such a catalytic social context, we will need to work against cultural prescriptions for older people. The strong individualism of our society comes to full flower in the way we conceive of the last third of life. Our cultural mind-set imagines elders moving off to the periphery of society as private individuals or as nuclear families. They may receive visitors occasionally or may possibly be consulted on this or that issue. But the golden years are perceived as a withdrawal from the active encounters of society. This isolating and fragmenting influence on elders diminishes their creative potential. If we do not consciously understand this cultural tendency and act against it, we will find ourselves bereft of exciting, demanding environments. We will find ourselves "out to pasture," the image of an animal grazing alone on distant fields. As elders, therefore, we need to seek out stimulating communities and plan a retirement linked to such surroundings. Contact with such communities, moreover, must satisfy both intellectual and emotional needs. Creativity is much more than a matter of intelligence; a very important quotient of affect enters into being a lively and contributing older person. Thus we need to be in dialogue with significant individuals and cultural settings that stimulate our minds. But we also require at the same time nurturing and supportive communities of friendship.

In brief, creativity in elderhood calls for a combination of personal traits cultivated in intellectual, artistic, and affective communities. The creative elder has gradually developed an independence of spirit, an active receptiveness to the holistic picture of reality, and a strong openness to ambiguity and complexity. He or she exercises these qualities for personal and social welfare in a network of supporting communities.

Prepare for this meditation by doing some deep breathing exercises. When you feel centered and tranquil, select a person, whether famous or known only to a few people, who strikes you as admirably creative. It would be preferable to choose an older person. Imagine this individual in the context of his or her life. Let your memory assist you as you see this person experiencing independent judgment and action. Mull over the traits of this independence of spirit. It is not a quality of adolescent rebellion by which a young person deviates from accepted norms to establish self-identity. Rather, you notice how the independence of thought or activity flows from the inner convictions of an established self-identity, one able to stand against conventional views. This independence also springs from the model's ability to experience inner feelings and insights.

Observe the way in which the imagined elder becomes receptive to a wider reality around him or her without forcing interpretations on things. If the interactions are in the realm of personal relationships, the model listens closely to what is said, how it is said, and looks carefully at the conduct of others. He or she wants to be able to make suggestions or decisions that are genuinely beneficial to others. This measure of creativity does not result from hastily projecting one's feelings and thoughts onto others. If the creative person's area should be in scientific fields, notice how patiently the figure allows natural, documentary, or laboratory evidence to reveal its secrets.

Imagine how the creative elder deals with a complex world of diverse structures, beliefs, and movements. He or she does not expect to have fully satisfying answers. But watch the person embrace complexity without attempting to oversimplify it with a hasty judgment. Ambiguous and even warring systems defy easy harmony in the realm of physical science and in human affairs. Try to imagine him or her in a concrete situation, dealing with conflict and uncertainty. What can you learn about creative attitudes as you imaginatively witness the person's responses?

What kind of supportive community both stimulates and upholds your model elder? See him or her surrounded by close friends or family. Perhaps a whole movement of people with kindred spirits, whether physically present or distant, gives this person courage and illumination. Or it may be that only a few teachers and supporters form a nucleus for creative endeavors.

As you conclude this meditation, let all these images flow freely through your mind. In reality, they all happen together, now with stress on one aspect, now on another. As you return to concentration on your breathing, do not strain to remember any of the images of this contemplation. They will be with you in whatever way is appropriate. As you inhale and exhale slowly, open yourself to whatever gifts of creativity can be yours, in keeping with your special personality, as you move toward elderhood.

BEING RELIGIOUS

Most people see themselves as religious or nonreligious in terms of affiliation with churches or synagogues. In the earlier tribal history of our species, there was much less distinction between sacred and secular life. But in the modern world, with it compartmentalization of functions and roles, religion generally refers to church buildings, clerical professionals, and specific practices. This understanding of religiousness is valid and important; yet it is always inadequate and misleading. For it tends to explain the spiritual dimension by external criteria, as though one's denomination represented the main story of one's religion. A more complete way of interpreting religiousness would interrelate the doctrine and morals of a particular church to the way a person truly believes and acts. In this sense, we talk about the seriousness of a person's convictions and how well he/she lives out a tradition's tenets. But an even richer appreciation of the religious spirit ties it intrinsically to our continuing encounter with the dilemmas of meaning and of ethical choice in our everyday life. This level of religiousness can certainly be related to traditional religions, but it is every bit as valuable even if it is not so related. We are pointing here to something basically human, that is, the quest for truth, for deeper experience of what is and what transcends us, for a more just and loving community.

The aging process influences this quest by putting us in touch with our own finitude and with many other challenges that are intrinsic to midlife and elderhood. As we encounter these problematic transition points on the life span, we are called upon to develop our own religiousness. Such personal religion may maintain many referents to a given historical tradition, but it is not completely defined or ruled by a specific religion. To develop one's own personal religiousness is no simple matter; it requires thoughtfulness, openness, self-scrutiny, and a spirit of risk and adventure. Yet we must avoid a kind of adolescent rejection of organized religion. This may happen because it fails to live up to exaggerated ideals, or because we have outgrown our scant knowledge of it, or simply because we have grown tired of religion as a burden from the past. As we develop our own religiousness, we will surely cherish wise and helpful lessons from our particular histories. But we will also understand our need to respond to the authentic questions springing from our own experiences. As we become our own spiritual guides, we may appear less faithful and observant to others. We will most likely manifest more critical attitudes toward commitments that we embraced in the past or toward doctrines that we believed without scrutiny. Yet we will trust our insights and judgments as we move further along the aging path.

We have referred to personal spirituality or religiousness as a quest for truth and right living. The dimension of truth connotes much more than just abstract knowledge; it involves an experiential journey toward meaning and purpose. What is the significance of our lives? What gives them value? Are we in communion with divine being in and beyond the world? Sometimes this quest is marked by special moments called mystical experiences. How does God make a difference for us? Is the journey of our own making only or are we inspired and carried forward by grace? How does this graciousness operate in a world that frequently appears indifferent to such searchings or destructive of them? We attempt to explore the meaning of religiousness through such queries, because genuine spirituality has less to do with inherited answers than with a personalized process of honest questioning. Again, these questions are not voiced in a vacuum;

rather they rise up from experiences of our own in everyday life as we confront specific challenges to us personally, to our families, and to society. Thus spirituality also signifies a quest for truth in ethical living. On this level, further questions spring up. Do we treat the persons closest to us with respect and benevolence? Do we act with integrity in our various involvements? How can we exercise responsibility for the larger social-ethical issues of justice, peace, and ecological care?

Religiousness, therefore, as the personal quest for truth and right living pervades an individual's whole life. Spirituality, or lack thereof, radiates from the way we live our everyday lives. It is primarily what goes on within ourselves and in our relations with others; only secondarily does religion concern religious organizations. The aging process at its best is a summons to pursue this journey toward a deeper, more excellent way of being human which also means being religious or spiritual. The paths lead inward and outward. Contemplation, whether in solitude or in company with others, allows our inner voices to speak. Sometimes this consists in listening carefully to images and stories carried to consciousness by our dreams and twilight reflections. At other times, interior meditation will attune us to the personalized meaning of a narrative or a doctrine deriving from a historical, spiritual movement. Medieval theologians spoke of carrying into the external world what we have contemplated within ourselves: *contemplata tradere*. The point here is the mutual interplay between the inner and outer roles in religiousness. While we are inspired by contemplation to understand ourselves and reach out in new ways to the world around us, we are also challenged by mundane events to search for truthful meaning and action. For example, the plight of the poor, the hungry, the sick, and the oppressed stirs our conscience toward spiritual/ethical conviction and involvement.

Just as there are diverse ways of experiencing one's religiousness within, so also outward expressions of spirituality will differ. Our religious sensibilities will be affected by differences in our education, temperament, even our age. Most of us in midlife and elderhood can recall modes of religiousness in our youth that are no longer appropriate for us. It is very helpful to realize that different personality types will be attracted to diverse forms of religious expression. Some will be quietly interior for the most part; others will engage principally in charismatic and liturgical involvements. When our spirituality inspires outward ethical concerns, different understandings of what conscience demands can become controversial. Some, like the liberation theologians, will advocate a thorough reform of political, social, and economic structures as a religious mandate. Others, such as many evangelical Christians, will encourage direct deeds of charity to the needy, but will argue against the reformation of institutions and society as a spiritual concern. The former group interprets the Bible in the light of social revolution; the latter movement fears such political entanglements as injurious to religiousness. These issues have been pursued at length in contemporary writing; the point for us is to recognize the diversity of outward experiences of the religious impulse. In many instances, diverse directions are mutually complementary. In some cases contradictory outward expressions of inner religious convictions can lead to profound disagreement and strong dispute. To moderate these clashes another aspect of authentic spirituality must enter the dialogue, namely, respect for the faith-convictions of others and an unflagging desire to uphold the personal dignity of those who disagree with us.

As you turn now to meditate on these issues, assume a comfortable but attention-supporting posture. Calm and center yourself with a few minutes of slow breathing exercises. You may want to turn the palms of both hands upward on your thighs as a gesture of openness and receptivity.

Contemplate first your whole person as innately religious. When you are ready, imagine a bright point of light located just inside your rib cage. The light is golden representing a search for wisdom, that combination of experience and healing knowledge. You notice that the circle of golden light also extends itself with bright rays in all directions, filling your entire body-person; the glow is also warm energy pulsating from the center outward. The light and heat radiate beyond the limits of your person; they encounter similar rays coming from different beings in the world. This symbolic picture mirrors our theme: religiousness resides deeply within you and in others; it penetrates all aspects of yourself in the quest for meaning and wisdom. Moreover, your spirituality expands outward to meet the religious energies of others in mutually enriching insights and in ethical involvements. You, as a microcosm of the universe, are a being of earth infused with spiritual light.

As a person in midlife or elderhood, you desire to realize daily and more concretely the call and challenge to dwell on the earth religiously. Go back in memory to your youth and recapture your understanding and expression of religiousness. Perhaps it was a rote exercise to please parents or other authorities. Maybe it was compartmentalized into a minor portion of your living experience. Or was it circumscribed by tedious roles and fearful admonitions? Yet there may also have been positive moments when the religion of childhood or youth already gave you glimpses of the all-encompassing world of spirit. Imagine these bright moments as the same golden light but seen at a great distance. It will appear tiny, like the headlight of a locomotive miles back down the track. As the light approaches, it grows larger and takes in the surrounding landscape. The track represents your life journey as you progress toward elderhood. Now you want to become more aware of the light as it illuminates the world around you, and as it lets you see what needs to be done by you.

Realize also that the light is given; it comes toward you; it was residing unseen within you. As a person of mind and body, you are called to enter into the light, to enjoy it, to take responsibility for it, to become its witness. Your vocation is to live as a human instrument of this growing, evolving illumination. The light is always endangered; it can be diminished by neglect and violence. The source of light also depends on you to be a custodian of its healing warmth and illumination. You have been given these scores of years not to bewail the loss of youth or to try to live by its distant glow. Rather the gift of years is bestowed so that you can be more deeply enlightened and become a beacon of healing illumination for the world.

·21

MAKING FRIENDS/ENEMIES

 A great goal in midlife and elderhood consists in the expansion of our circle of friends and in the deepening of certain friendships. This meditation on friends and enemies centers on the problems of love and hate, major forces that either open people to spiritual development in their mature years or close them into bitterness and suspicion. Weekly news magazines testify on page after page that the world around us is filled with hatred and animosity. We would be naïve to proclaim that simple remedies could cure the hostility and violence of humanity. We would distort the truth if we overlooked personal and social conditions that do injustice to many persons and to classes in society, disposing them to hate enemies. Yet the summons to spiritual maturity in the aging process calls us to explore the roots of our own animosities. If we would grow in wisdom and graciousness, we must ask ourselves why we hate, or if that word is too strong, why we hold grudges and ill feelings toward specific persons and whole groups.

Much of our hatred stems from fear, and fear flows from deep insecurity. We fear and feel hostile toward that which seems to threaten us. Again, much depends on our earlier experiences of trust and security. All of us bear significant anxiety from childhood, although much of it may be unconsciously buried under layers of repression or suppression. It may take us years to recognize this insecurity about our identity, our worthiness, our survival. If we were blessed with caring parents, we may find ourselves on the less fearful end of the spectrum of anxiety about threats from others. We will have a head start, as it were, in facing our anxieties and also in reaching out to others in friendship. But many people are severely injured by early insecurities that tend to be compounded by later hurts from individuals or groups.

Unfortunately, it is easier for such persons to make enemies than to cultivate friendships. Not that this is done consciously; they would probably not rationally admit such a negative tendency. But reflect for a moment on the deeper needs of enemy-makers. In a kind of distorted way, they feel more secure by isolating other persons, institutions, or movements as enemies, as threats to their fragile security. If the enemy can be defined and located, a certain sense of wellbeing results. Not being able to name the sources of one's anxieties leads to a pervasive sense of terror and even paranoia. Again, on a conscious level, such people desire friendships; they can attest to the values of having friends. But at a more powerful, usually unperceived level of motivation, the need for enemies wins out; friends can't be trusted. Don't the injuries of the past confirm this?

We might erroneously conclude from what has been said that no enemies exist. They are only of our making. Not at all. Surely, dangerous people, twisted and dehumanized in their own formative environments, threaten our welfare. Society must take measures to guard against such destructiveness. Moreover, whole movements can assume demonic force, as for example, the Nazis in our own era. This meditation does not seek to summon us toward Pollyanna thinking in our mature years. It is precisely realism that urges us to look hard at our tendency to unnecessarily create enemies, thus increasing the world's destructive potential. This becomes abundantly clear in the case of most wars. To motivate young men to wreak terrible violence on another group of humans, leaders typically dehumanize the latter as vicious enemies. Such enemies become a pseudospecies, less than human. Therefore, it becomes good to kill them. Choose your warring situation and you will find this psychological mechanism at work. Iran–Iraq, Israeli–Palestinian, Irish Protestant–Catholic—extend the list at will; the enemy-making mechanism rolls on. Sometimes religious and/or political ideology lubricates its wheels; at other times, real injustices and oppression spark its engines. But whatever the provocation, our earliest insecurities are touched and our all-too-ready penchant to make enemies is activated. It is extremely difficult for us to distinguish between the injustice and its perpetrator, between the sin and the sinner. We lump such elements together as the enemy to avoid or to attack.

Making friends is also a demanding task. On the personal level, we usually experience a certain affinity of temperament, interests, and outlook with a friend. This provides us with a basis for building a relationship of trust and delight in one another's company. Of course, friends can disagree, even strongly, but the differences are not allowed to poison the wellsprings of affection and general mutuality. With the responsibilities of midlife it is easy to neglect personal friendships. Yet making and cultivating friendships is one of the most important dimensions of creative aging. Friends from our past keep alive the memories of our significant, formative experiences. These friends become for us the living threads of continuity in our life tapestry. They sustain us in the present as we weave together the new strands of our story. By sharing our key experiences, close friends become more than any one of them could be without the friendship. For friends live mutually within one another; this inner presence of the friend within expands our world and our existence.

When our friendship moves to the zone of intimacy, new dangers lie in waiting. The very uniqueness of this type of bonding and its intensity of emotional commitment tap our deepest fears, expectations, and longings. Those most vulnerable areas of our private selves, not generally disturbed by companionate friendships, are at stake in the intimate relationship. Here it is that we can do the deepest healing or harming. Of course it is not our intention to explore these friendships at length; a sizeable and worthwhile literature already exists. Our point is rather to underscore the subtle dynamics of these friendships. They constitute one of the best ways to overcome our early insecurities and foster our full development. But friendships, especially on the intimate level, can also turn to inimical encounters that blight our souls, making us more fearful, depressed, and suspicious, in a word, more inclined to see enemies all around.

Friendship calls for open and benevolent communication at every level, although the modes of expression will differ. As we gradually overcome our insecurity-based defensiveness, we can be more open in speaking truth to others and in hearing the truth spoken to us. Deeper friendship is not possible without authentic communication. Just as good exchange is the essential milieu of a friendship, so benevolence warms its core. The Italian expression for loving another, *ti voglio bene*, literally, "I wish you well," underlines the importance of benevolence better than "I love you." The best friendships, whether in a marriage or in other relationships, flow from desiring the welfare of the other. Such love transcends romantic feelings not only in its durability but also by its intrinsic value.

Openness and benevolence, furthermore, characterize the best aspects of friendship on the social level. To be open means to understand those of different cultures and creeds on their own terms, as much as possible. Disagreement with the ways of other groups is consistent with such an attitude. What matters is how we differ. Do we listen from a basically closed mind, having already categorized other races, nations, religions as perverse and threatening? In the guise of dialogue, have we already labeled them as an irremediable pseudospecies? Or do we move from true openness toward benevolence? Desiring the wellbeing of other groups will not of itself alter historical wrongs and change present structures of injustice and oppression. But a genuine care for the good of other peoples, especially those who live under oppressive conditions or those we have been told to regard as enemies, will shape us into true cultivators of human friendship. Midlife and elderhood offer a special time to make friendship, on individual and group levels, one of the highest priorities.

Place yourself in a comfortable but firm seat for this meditation. Do some preliminary breathing exercises to calm and center yourself. Draw into your imagination concrete images of a few persons you dislike. Perhaps celebrities will come to mind; or you may focus on a personal acquaintance or relative. The purpose of this meditation is not to make you feel guilty for negative sentiments toward others. Let the feelings be what they are; no need to force them to be any other way. Rather our aim is to distinguish as best we can between solid reasons for disliking this person and our own fears or insecurities that drive us to manufacture enemies. As you quietly watch the individual speak and act in characteristic ways, ask yourself what it is that bothers you most about the person. Do you find any traces of such traits in yourself? Perhaps the disliked image dramatizes aspects you decry in yourself but have not changed.

Or it may be that this enemy figure expresses negative qualities that are not part of you, traits that you rightly reject. In this case, can you separate the negative characteristics from the basic personality of the other? If you can make this distinction, dwell on the lovable dimension of the other. If you cannot separate trait from basic personality in the other, first admit this to yourself. Then, while acknowledging the possibility of error, own the negative sentiment toward the other as a genuine feeling in you – a feeling not dictated mainly by defensive motives stemming from your own insecurities. As an aging individual, you want to avoid as consciously as you can negative feelings toward others that are based solely on unexamined reflex reactions in yourself. You are seeing more clearly that such defensiveness isn't needed and, moreover, that it impedes your full human development.

Shift your contemplative focus to groups toward which you sense antipathy. It may be a whole nation or a political or social movement; perhaps a religious or cultural organization comes to mind. Choose the one that seems to arouse the strongest negative feeling at present. Imagine as specifically as you can what its members do, how they speak, what values undergird their movement. Let your real sentiments arise; to suppress them for some ideal purpose only postpones the needed encounter with these feelings. Can you center on the principal feeling toward these people? Is it envy, contempt, fear, hostility, or outright hatred? Try to determine the nature of your feeling, experience it, and just let it be. Now return to the group you have singled out. Does your negative assessment attach to these people in everything they do or propose? As you watch them again, see if you notice some activities or modes of speaking during a typical day that you could admire. Perhaps they are considerate and generous to their families; they may help an important charity or donate time and energy to a tutorial project for the less privileged. As you contemplate this side of the disliked group, allow and own any positive feelings that surface, feelings that you never thought possible toward these persons. You are permitting your inner self to balance itself, to fashion a more nuanced set of attitudes toward the "enemy" group. You are also disposing yourself toward creative growth as you age. As a mature person, you are sufficiently secure not to need or to create enemies; you understand that a more complex view of disliked groups will lessen violent sentiments in your psyche and in the world.

Conclude your meditation by using the words "openness" and "benevolence" as mantras. As you breathe slowly and deeply, imagine your inhaled breath as a gentle taking in of the world as it is with openness. You must eventually distinguish between what you consider good and evil, but let the first moment be one of kindly acceptance without prejudgment. As you exhale, let the feelings of benevolence flow out of you and gather like a healing mist around individuals and groups that you have disliked. Do this exercise for a few minutes as a way of preparing your own spirit for growth toward an elderhood of expanding friendliness.

22

CHANGING TOWARD MEANING/VALUE

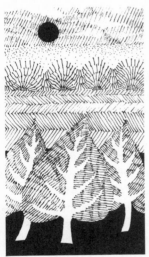

Aging implies change. On the physical level, the process of change strikes us most clearly. We see dramatic differences in a photographic history of an individual from childhood to elderhood. We quickly and almost unconsciously categorize people into general age groups according to their physical traits. We are sometimes amazed by how much a friend may have changed in bodily appearance if we have not seen the individual for a long time. We also observe change in the psychological realm when we speak of maturity or new attitudes. We refer to the young adults as mature because they take on responsibilities they were not capable of in childhood. Or we notice that an old friend has shifted her attitude in the political or social sphere. Furthermore, society teaches us to connect aging with change. Many forms of legislation concerning retired and other elderly people influence our outlook; we tend to classify older persons in a group where significant changes have occurred. They are seen as beyond their working years, experiencing a less demanding life-style, and possibly in need of special care and protection. Yet these physical, psychological, and societal alterations may easily miss the most important changes.

These concern questions of meaning and value. What changing has taken place as we grow older on the deeper plane of our philosophy of life and our ethical/aesthetic involvements? How have we changed spiritually over the years?

Before we look directly at growth in meaning and values, we should ask about how much we actually can and do change. While many people seem uninterested in the changes needed to develop their potential, others expect too much change. The latter engage in an unfortunate flight from human limitations. They anticipate all manner of therapeutic possibilities that only serve to inflate the ego or produce discouragement through unfulfilled or dashed expectations. Exaggerated claims about human potential from astral travel to extraordinary psychic feats add to the ways by which we deny our finitude and mortality. On a somewhat less "magical" level, a good number of religious preachers and therapeutic gurus assure us of marvelous personality changes if we follow their prescriptions. The former advance a type of instant transformation through religious conversion. Converts describe great changes in conduct and attitude from the "before" to the "after" stages of conversion. The new psychological converts can point to radical shifts in lifestyle as they renounce conventional Western mores to live in communes under the dictates of a leading guru. But a long-term study of these individuals would probably disclose less dramatic changes on the levels of personality and spirituality. Finally, not all change is desirable; we do well to scrutinize and perhaps resist certain proposed changes.

How much can we really change in the aging process? It is important to recognize certain givens that limit or strongly condition modes of personal development. Our particular genetic components circumscribe and influence our potential for growth on intellectual, emotional, and physical levels. Our talents and basic temperament will always shape our lives within certain parameters. Moreover, our earliest childhood experiences mark us for life in certain important ways. Our basic ability to trust and accept ourselves with reference to the world results from our early development of confidence in a parental milieu. Secondary traits of nervousness and anxiety can also be traced to the interplay of one's own genetic dispositions with the influences of the earliest family context.

We can certainly change as we move through life, affected by the many influences and opportunities that are distinctly personal to us. But most of us are quite amazed in midlife by how difficult it is to alter the early programing of childhood, especially certain ways of acting or thinking that we now judge as negative. To be aware of these limits of change can be helpful in two ways. It protects us against disillusionment after we have followed various techniques for spiritual/humanistic growth, only to find the same old traits cropping up. The consciousness of our limits also reveals the uniqueness of our mind, emotions, and spirituality. We must develop in ways that are proper to our own personality type with its peculiar dispositions. Certain teachings, teachers, and practices will be more appropriate for us than for others along the path toward wholeness. In brief, we can change our thinking, feeling, and behavior in keeping with genetic dispositions and early childhood experiences.

But what sort of change leads to fulfillment in the aging sequence? It is the changing or development that brings about the most inspiring and beautiful vision of human existence (meaning) that is capable of energizing consonant affections, choices, and valuable actions. The realm of meaning is sometimes referred to as one's philosophy of life. Such are the ideals or goals that constitute a person's deepest levels of enlightenment and motivation to live virtuously. Virtues are those qualities or dispositions of mind and heart that exemplify meaning in action; more on this when we consider values. To fashion a vision of meaning is an ongoing task; change is normal and instrinsic to it. Many influences bear at one time and successively on the shaping of one's horizon of meaning. Recall just a few of these: parents, siblings, friends, teachers, traumatic or wonderful life happenings, religious and humanistic environments. Yet this context or horizon of meaning may undergo particular turmoil at different stages of the life span. Older meaning patterns can fall apart for many reasons, such as inadequate insight into an otherwise meaningful tradition when new periods of life elicit unmet crises. Or encounters with different meaning systems may shake assurances that encircled an earlier network of meaning. Such crises impel us to choose or settle for lesser meaning systems or to struggle toward reformulating a broader horizon, integrating into it aspects of the challenging meaning system. In the pluralistic encounters of the contemporary world, we are continuously invited to reformulate our context of meaning. Christians, Buddhists, Jews, Marxists, socialists, capitalists, democrats, totalitarians, and many others present competing, sometimes complementary systems of meaning. Where do we stand personally in shaping our own horizon of meaning?

This is a question about our ideals and goals. Perhaps we never ask ourselves such queries. Rather we move along automatically day by day without meditating on life goals. This course may appear easier to us, but it almost always means that we live unconsciously according to the unperceived goals and ideals of the general culture. Conventional ideas of the media tend to formulate our horizon for us. We are carried along by a common popular flow; we do not plan and shape our own existence. More people today embrace planning for the future in such areas as career options, financial investments, and retirement planning. Yet the same persons seem quite oblivious to formulating plans for their full human fulfillment in midlife and elderhood. They mistakenly believe that the attainment of material, occupational, and perhaps familial goals signifies the development of their fullest potential as psychospiritual beings. No great mosaic of beauty was ever built without an overall design, whether as abstract or representational art. If our lives are to become a mosaic of beauty, we need to draft some preliminary sketches, subject to revision as our goals become clearer. It is never too late to envision the overall design of one's mosaic starting with the pieces most familiar to oneself.

When we speak of shaping a horizon of meaning for ourselves as we proceed along the aging spectrum, we must speak also of values, as these are concretely chosen and lived. Meaning or horizon represents the end or goal; values as existentially embraced are the means that carry us toward these goals. While it is useful to discuss such relationships in a conceptual way, it will be more rewarding for us to study meaning and values as these meld together in specific individuals who can become models for our own journeys. We do not want slavishly to imitate one or more model figures. This would deny our own uniqueness and ultimately hinder our development. But certain persons past and present incorporate in their lives a mixture of virtues that facilitate becoming old. Of course none of these famous individuals set out to achieve some preconceived goal totally of their own making. This would be a distortion of the process of change toward a more excellent horizon.

Great models of human existence believed that the goals were gradually revealed to them as they tried to live out values for their own sake. This was true for Jesus and Francis, for Maimonides and Mohammed as well as for many other spiritual men and women throughout the ages. The holy people of the East like Gotama and Gandhi incarnated values of wisdom and compassion in ways that enrich the visions and practices of the West. If we speak of our heroes, we manifest our highest ideals. But such horizons remain abstract until we actually walk the path of virtues exemplified by a master spirit. We greatly underestimate our spiritual capacity; we are all potential mystics and saints. We might make models of more recent figures, perhaps even contemporaries. In many realms of value, there will also be secular personalities. Such women and men of high integrity, courage, and vision are "secular" in that they are not chiefly associated with a specific religious tradition; but when we look more closely at the ways of justice, hope, and charity demonstrated in their lives, these persons, too, qualify as deeply spiritual models.

Now that we have reflected on limits and potentials for change in the aging process, we move into the meditation itself. After settling ourselves quietly in our special place for contemplation, we will do a set of breathing exercises. As we prepare to meditate through spiritual dialogue with a chosen hero, let us remember that each one of these models struggled with some of the challenges of midlife and possibly even elderhood. Their roads to deepened meaning and lived values traversed the doubts, handi-

caps, and other challenges that face us. Their paths were circui-
tous and sometimes misleading; by persistence and resiliency
they climbed a road toward higher levels of human consciousness and interaction. Remember, too, that exemplars do not
have to be perfect in all ways to act as guides for change in the
aging journey.

Choose an individual who attracts you as an ideal of the search
for meaning and value in life. This man or woman may be a his-
toric figure or a modern person. Let him or her appear as graphi-
cally as possible in your pictorial imagination. Notice how this
revered figure looks, moves, talks. Now you are going to approach this model to learn what you can about changing to realize your potential. Imagine that both of you are seated facing
one another in a quiet, beautiful garden. The admirable person
greets you gently by name, asking if he or she can be of service
to you. Pause for a few moments, let yourself feel at ease with
this imaginary guest, and decide what questions you want to
ask about meaning and value.

You may wish to begin by asking how your guide developed a
powerfully motivating philosophy of life. The answers would
almost certainly cause you to review the significant life experiences of this person. The horizon of meaning would have emerged
from the particular encounters with other individuals and events,
as well as with the person's own private realm of reflection and
meditation. Allow your imagination and your own experience
of life to carry you across the gaps in your knowledge of your
model. Listen now to your inner visitor as he or she recounts
some of these major experiences. As you attend to the responses,
you group them according to events of childhood and youth,
midlife, and possibly elderhood in that individual's life span.
Give yourself time to repeat to yourself key phrases from this
discourse that indicate milestones along the road of the model's
growth toward fuller meaning. It may be sufficient to repeat to
yourself, as if they were a mantra, particular names, events,
movements that deeply influenced your spiritual mentor. Stay
with this exercise of mental absorption; his or her experiences
are being vicariously transferred to your own growing network
of meaning.

After dwelling on his or her philosophy of life, you want to explore more closely with your guest the specific virtues or values that were the lived means of approaching such excellent horizons. In imagination reconstruct the scenes of your guide's model actions. Perhaps images of courageous action or empathetic, compassionate dealings come to mind. Witness your model in trying situations; observe the truthful and respectful ways by which the mentor responds. Your hero strives, as much as possible, to preserve the dignity of opponents and to sustain the spirits of companions. See how he or she copes with psychological and physical suffering; you may notice no defensive anger at seeming threats to his or her ego; perhaps you will perceive a note of humor in response to physical disabilities. Continue for a while to let such scenes of value play themselves out before you.

In the end, you reach out both hands, grasping the outstretched hands of your mentor. Without words or new images, you simply open yourself to the silent flow of the guide's spirit into you. With gratitude you experience this spirit of meaning and value adapting itself to you as you age toward greater wisdom and love.

23

TRANSFORMING WORK

Our attitude toward work will strongly affect the journey toward realizing our potential in the aging process. People spend a great portion of their lives at the workplace – the best hours of the day, from Monday to Friday, for as much as fifty years. For many, work becomes the most important shaping influence for self-identity. Individuals may not like what they do, but they mainly define themselves by the nature of their occupations. Modern studies underscore the widespread dissatisfaction with one's job. On the lower echelons of the economic scale, workers often complain about boredom, lack of respect and dignity, insufficient rewards, poor conditions, and the prospect of a dreary future trapped in the same type of employment. Others wish they could find alternative ways to make a living, but age, lack of options, self-doubt, and fear of being jobless cause them to plod along daily in quiet, sometimes desperate resignation.

In the upper levels of our reward system, persons are even more prone to identify their self-worth and social status with occupational or professional success. But here, too, much discontent prevails. Seemingly successful individuals express unhappiness with their work. If they have achieved certain occupational goals, they may discover a disappointment concerning earlier expectations. They find themselves running ever harder to compete in a race for which they have secretly lost real interest. This condition which so many experience results in a psychological tearing apart, a kind of low-level schizophrenia: to appear to like what demands so much of them while strongly disliking the work at deeper levels of the personality. The ostensibly less successful members of the more educated classes experience a heightened sense of failure. In their eyes and according to the criteria of a money-power society, they suffer psychological devaluation. Apathy and routine carry them along in the workplace; real interests have to be squeezed into the brief hours on the fringes of the job. Open or hidden stress generated in these common situations will have a negative impact on mental and physical wellbeing.

The accumulated dissatisfaction with lives identified with such work may be reflected in the dramatic statistics that a quarter of American suicides involve white males over sixty-five. And these figures represent only the tip of the iceberg of job-related unhappiness in elderhood. Some will look back on their working careers only to see failure because they lacked the courage or the opportunity to pursue authentic desires. Others will have so thoroughly identified their self-worth with an occupational role, whether truly chosen or not, that retirement from such work renders them useless castaways in their own minds. An even stronger phrase in our culture than "you are what you eat" is "you are what you do" (in the worksphere). The first group of self-described failures alerts us to the vital need to examine the quality and appropriateness of one's job early in life. We are also moved to search for means of transforming our attitudes toward work, whatever it may be. The second group who attached all personal value to their social role inspires us to explore other ways of understanding our worth and vocation in life. This whole picture is further complicated in our time by the greatly increased entry of women into the workplace. How will the younger career woman balance her various identities in creative ways as she ages? How can the older woman wisely approach the workworld after many years of domestic engagement?

In light of these problems, what steps can be taken to transform our work into a creative process? If we are simply putting in time, watching the clock, or waiting for the whistle, we waste many of the best years of our life. Or we might perform our tasks routinely, with a modicum of satisfaction, without seriously exploring the relationship between our jobs and our growth as persons, our development toward the wisdom and compassion of elderhood. Jung gave us an important expression of an ideal relationship between work and spiritual growth when he spoke of his whole psychological enterprise, covering more than half a century, as a series of milestones along his personal journey. His own human development and his work as a psychologist reciprocally nourished each other. Such an ideal situation escapes most people because of the nature of their work, the level of their education in self-reflection, but perhaps most of all, because of their attitude toward their jobs.

Yet even Jung's attitude toward his profession must not be seen as a smooth, trouble-free ascent toward personal wholeness. Various profound crises challenged his inner life, while external events, especially the early history of his relations with Freud, deeply shook his confidence concerning his place in the psychological movement. After a serious examination of how our work impinges on our lives, we may need to decide about alternative courses to take. For those under great stress in the marketplace, a major shift may be necessary. B. F. Skinner, in his recent reflections on creative aging, suggests altering the environment of one's work. If family or other repsonsibilities preclude any significant job change, forming a new attitude toward one's work can assist self-development and inner peace. Again, Jung advises us well when he invites us to learn to see differently a task we may not be able to change. Nor is this merely a counsel for resignation in face of the inevitable. On the contrary, the kind of transformation implied in "seeing differently" affects all work, even that which is gratifying. Older people can also prepare themselves to do what they would find more enjoyable, whether as avocation or vocation.

To transform the meaning of our work, we must undergo more than just a change of mind. Rather, a deeper emotional-spiritual transformation, the sort that is particularly appropriate to middle age, can gradually revise our attitude toward daily tasks. One of the principal aspects of this transformation is the authentic, inward appropriation of an attitude of enabling others to grow. This does not mean giving up our own pleasures and the desire for reward through work. But the new attitude entails a profound change of priorities. The main emphasis is not self-gratification or the enhancement of the power of dominance over others. We learn to find genuine joy in fostering the true welfare of others as individuals and in communities. For some of these empowering contributions will be more physical, having to do with goods and services. For others, enabling power will more directly influence the education of minds and hearts. Further dimensions of this new outlook involve a change from a mainly competitive to a cooperative stance in reference to one's job. Cooperation does not necessarily signify conformity and compliance; the cooperative spirit may call for strongly opposing majority views or even standing up against a particular program or individual at costly risks to self. Work becomes an occasion for giving more than for taking, for sharing rather than for amassing things for oneself. Some will question whether such a spiritual conversion of heart is truly possible, given our human proclivity toward self-interested actions. Others will look upon it as a self-justifying and self-gratifying rationalization merely cloaking basic human greed.

Yet this enabling spirit toward one's work and toward life in general is both possible, authentic, and vitally necessary for self and society. The dominant view in our acquisitive culture holds that humans act from self-interest and not from altruism. Of course, personal reward is a major motivation of our endeavors. But not enough attention is given to altruism as a satisfying motive in the marketplace. Just as one can rightly speak of self-interest as natural in light of our insecurities and our desire for valuation, so also can we understand altruism as natural. The animal realm widely manifests a kind of instinctive altruism when dolphins come to one another's aid in dangerous situations. Many examples of mutual help and even sacrificial conduct can be found in nature from the interactions of the smallest organisms

to the complex rituals of primates. When the Buddha emphasized the profound interconnectedness of all reality, he was not
announcing some alien theory. When Francis of Asissi's prayer
tells us "For it is in giving that we receive," he points to a deep
human truth. The transformation of our work into cooperative
and altruistic modes is a needed corrective to the unhealthy
mentality that sees the workplace as an arena for the exercise of
unbridled self-interest. Physical and mental health for individuals and groups depends to an important extent on the lessening
of stress and fragmentation arising from a "dog-eat-dog" work
ethos. The enabling spirit holds a vital key to creative aging in
midlife and elderhood.

As you do preliminary breathing exercises for centering yourself in meditation, notice how interlinked and reciprocal the
simplest motions of life are. Look at the taken-for-granted workplace of your physical-mental organism. The major systems of
life are working in tandem, helping one another for the good of
the whole. Lungs work to draw in blood-nourishing oxygen from
the outer world of nature. Your heart pumps the reenergized
blood through arteries to sustain cells throughout your body.
Complex neurological systems act like splendid computers acti-
vating and regulating the many networks that operate in unison.
Such harmony is actually more natural than the competitive,
isolated stressful mechanisms we humans have erected in our
civilization. Contemplating our natural rhythms gives us needed
perspective on the worth of cooperation and altruism in our
workworld.

As we age, we want to call into question the harmful patterns
that keep us from transforming work into creative, enabling
expression for ourselves and for our communities. The first
step is intelligent scrutiny. Let the typical pattern of a working
day pass across your imaginative screen. Notice obstacles from
the work itself, from associates, from your own way of approaching and programming work. Do the tasks themselves have merit
for you and for others? Is there obstruction from colleagues?
Filter out the true problem area and ask yourself if there may be

a remedy. Answers to such questions cannot be prescribed from outside; they will well up gradually from the silent depths of your meditation. What is it about your own approach to work that causes undue stress and blocks enjoyment? This last aspect may be the most important of all. Picture yourself at home in the morning getting ready to leave for work; what are your usual emotions and expectations? What is your attitude to the daily tasks as they occur? Is it a sense of pride and pleasure in handling a challenge well? Remember, the goal of this discernment is not to burden yourself further with guilt or "oughts." Rather, its purpose is to let go of obstacles to joy and creativity just as you expel tainted breath in exhaling. Actively imagine that this process of letting-go gradually purifies you of negative elements in your attitudes toward work.

In the concluding part of this meditation, return to your mantra. As you slowly repeat the special sound for centering and healing, let it surround and penetrate the images of your world of work. Pass before your imagination and memory the people, events, and places connected with your occupation. With each change of scene let the sound of the mantra fill the picture. Some images will elicit the negative emotions that you have learned to associate with them. Yet as you envelop these challenging scenes with the song of your mantra, you are permitting transformative energies to change your perception of the situation. It may be that you will see new opportunities for growth in circumstances that before offered only dead ends. On the other hand, the mantra experience may produce in you the courageous energy to move away from a debilitating job to seek more rewarding work. If you are beyond retirement age, the mantra/ work exercise can dispose your mind to search out new and creative ways to serve others with your talents.

As people of faith, we understand that our work in the world participates in the divine energies. God works in and through us to build communities of justice and peace where people can develop their potential while respecting and protecting the wider ecosystem of our planet. We may not see the results of such divine-human collaboration. Yet we occasionally get glimpses of our small efforts transformed into wider purposes than we had ever imagined.

·24

PEACEMAKING ELDERS

That we live in a terribly violent society does not require much proof. Turn the pages of a major urban newspaper for one week and the full panoply of human destructiveness appears. By violence we do not mean the assertiveness and even aggressiveness that are called for in various circumstances. Rather, violence represents that whole spectrum of destructive conduct from suicide and domestic cruelty to terrorism and warfare. This violence is both physical and psychological, individual and social, overt as in direct criminal attacks and covert as in institutional or structural injustices. What does all this have to do with aging? From a religious perspective, it has everything to do with aging. Consider the ideal growth pattern over a life span in Christianity and Buddhism. In neither spiritual movement are we encouraged to progress toward an elderhood of material wealth and power for the protection or expansion of our own narrow interests. The spirit of the Beatitudes envisions elders who, having undergone the evangelical revolution of mind and heart, dedicate themselves to reconciling hostile alienations at all levels of existence. Blessed are the peacemakers. The Bodhisattva image in Mahayana Buddhism presents the vision of an enlightened person who delays entry into bliss to exercise compassion toward all creatures with whom he or she feels intimately bound. Both of these ideals lift up peacemaking as a major goal of our life journey.

Before we return to this ideal as a focus of meditation, let us explore in more depth the roots of violence in the human soul. Although the causes of destructiveness are varied and complex, they can be thought about under two general headings: interior and exterior. From the springboard of our childhood insecurities, we approach the world as a more or less threatening place. Before any reflective awareness, we develop hostility when our self-worth or physical existence seem to be menaced. The word "seem" is crucial; to the degree that we feel threatened by persons and events, to the extent that our ego identity seems to be diminished or destroyed, we strike out in numerous ways to protect ourselves. Some of this defensiveness is a normal reaction; but many of the interiorized patterns for trying to maintain self-worth wreak havoc all around us.

Social learning and social injustices further cultivate our personal inclinations toward destructive conduct. Thus interior and exterior causes for violence reciprocally stimulate each other. We learn destructive modes of dealing with perceived threats and anxieties by imitating certain conduct in our social milieu. Models of violence, whether blatant or subtle, appear to be rewarded by various satisfactions. Add to this personal and cultural matrix for destructiveness political-economic-racial structures of oppression and injustice. The mixture of all these elements becomes extremely explosive; we can develop into walking time bombs ready to injure ourselves and others.

Of course, we can think of many nuances and variations on this theme. But ask yourself when do you feel most prone to strong anger or even violent behavior? Is it not when you perceive your basic worth or your physical existence threatened and diminished? Or perhaps you experience the same diminishment of personhood vicariously by association with oppressed groups. If we say that people act violently to gain material possessions, power over others, and self-aggrandizing fame, we are right. But the further question remains: Why do violent people want these things or outcomes? Is it not in the end that they are bolstering their inner security against diminishments and from an exterior standpoint are repeating socially learned patterns?

Midlife and elderhood present particularly rich periods for going inward to explore the sources of our own violent tendencies. We have lived long enough to be tired of and unconvinced by self-justifying rationalizations for our angry, hurtful conduct. We may have matured sufficiently to stop blaming our destructive ways exclusively on parental patterning or the evils of society. In other words, we as aging persons are willing to take responsibility for searching out and correcting the inner mechanism of our own violence. This first step of interior scrutiny is crucial for those who would respond wisely to the summons of older age to become peacemakers. If we do not appreciate in a very experiential mode our own patterns of destructive anger, we will not understand violence in others, and we will not be transformed into exemplary reconcilers of conflicts. This inner task can be aided by studying quality literature about the psychological dimensions of destructive behavior. Individual or group counseling will personalize what is learned in books. In the therapeutic enterprise we grasp in a lively, memorable manner how concepts of anger and violence have been concretely patterned from our earliest family experiences. In this area, the dream-and-waking journal can be especially significant. Dreams, for example, frequently mirror inner conflictual situations with repeated clusters of emotional reactions. These scenes can become vital landmarks on the road to interior discovery.

Aging persons who personally desire to understand both quiet and explosive styles of violent behavior must examine their domestic and possibly occupational life. Those tied to us emotionally, those who know us without our cultural masks, become the main catalysts for drawing forth our worst side. However much we theorize about growth toward a spirit of peace and reconciliation, a most revealing litmus test of our progress is domestic relations. By middle age we may be ready for serious dialogue about personal family affairs. Perhaps the experience of past failed relationships sensitizes us to this need. Or the prolonged fruitlessness of negative interaction with one's spouse or children can motivate the forty-five year old to review this network of interactions. Again, the older person may be secure enough about this or her personal identity and worth to risk exposing and taking responsibility for vulnerabilities. Of course, for optimal success, such communication toward greater respect and peace requires the willingness of all parties. Yet even if one partner seeks light on these issues, a transformation of understanding and even action becomes possible. As we approach elderhood, the family and the workplace provide truly important loci for growth as reconciling peacemakers. There, after all, are the places of concrete encounters with others where we can model and thus teach modes of conflict resolution and peaceful interaction.

The word "peace" calls for brief explanation as we reflect on the third realm of peacemaking, the societal. Peace is too often understood as a quiescent, immobile state. All seems silent; not much moves in the popular overtones of the term "peace." Or it conveys a negative meaning of no war. Some of these aspects belong to peace, but others must also be emphasized for an authentic understanding. Peace as *shalom* signifies dynamic interrelationships on personal and social levels. A peaceful situation may, and usually does, include conflict, diversity of opinions, and energetic expression of emotion. Peace mainly calls for a network of justice with respect for human rights and dignity. It is in this context that an older person functions as peacemaker. We do not expect the world to be a placid environment without challenge or peril. But the elder who has brought some inner reconciliation to his or her fears and threats will be in a position to recognize real menaces to peaceful relations in society. Our longer experience of social inequities and deprivations will alert us to great dangers for future human welfare. In our own nation, we will see the seeds sown for criminal and other forms of violence in the emotionally, physically, and intellectually brutalized childhoods of so many. At home and abroad we will observe with empathy and dissatisfaction the irony, the incongruity, of great wealth amid great poverty. We will grasp with sharper vision the structural evils that are accentuated by religious, ethnic, and nationalistic enmities. It is in this realistic context of actual and potential violence that we are summoned to become agents of *shalom*. Not by simple solutions or by grandiose gestures will peacemaking happen. Rather the elder who knows some peace within will gather with others to foster *shalom* in one or other area of principal need.

We turn to our meditation on peacemaking by assuming the usual quiet position and doing the breathing exercises. As you breathe in, imagine the inhaled air as a calming, nourishing element. Just as a peacemaker is a bridge builder, so breathing establishes a bridge between your unique self and all the rest of the external world. In this sense, breathing is a dialogical activity; nature is the partner that is drawn from outside the self to satisfy and sustain the integrity of the inner person. This reflection, while continuing the concentration on breathing, speaks directly to our first point: to be at peace with yourself. As aging persons we know from experience that achievements, fame, power, and wealth cannot produce inner peace, the accepting and loving of our true selves. Here we are also at the central point of understanding our inclination toward destructiveness. Because we love ourselves so little, because we are so little at peace with ourselves, we tend to lash out intentionally, verbally, even physically at whatever threatens to diminish us. Much violence stems from an unpeaceful soul. As you exhale, let the feelings of threat to your basic personhood flow out from you. As you draw in a new breath, imagine this new air enlivening the many aspects of your basic worth. As your indrawn breath fills your lungs and is carried by your bloodstream to the rest of your body, let it help to envigorate your unique qualities of mind, body, emotion, and spirit. These God-given blessings are yours regardless of society's judgments. Be at peace with the values that are you; no need to be threatened, to be defensively or offensively violent. From the firm foundation of your worth, you are moving toward an elderhood of peacemaking.

Now gently draw into the circle of your breathing the persons who are closest to you, most likely your own spouse, children, and special friends. Let each one pass before the eye of your inner mind. Each is a distinct, lovable person with needs and desires. Most of our angry or even violent sentiments toward these individuals arise because we feel either threatened or diminished by them or because we have not learned to let them be themselves as truly diverse persons. Of course, we have special responsibilities to set limits, counsel, and guide children. We also need to find ways of communicating honestly and kindly with adult loved ones. But domestic violence, psychological and physical, could be greatly curbed by convincing ourselves of two points: We are not to be easily threatened and we will allow the other to be truly other. Such an achievement bespeaks a high degree of maturity; we must not be discouraged if it does not happen overnight. Old patterns of feeling and communication resist change. But inasmuch as we can love ourselves enough not to feel easily diminished and respect the individuality of others, we will lessen destructive responses. Our communities of intimacy and friendship constitute the best school for learning to be peacemakers. Determine in this meditation that such a spirit of self-respect and other-respect shall characterize your aging process. The more you are able to implement this spirit, the more you will be enabled to communicate with honesty and care.

Finally, imagine yourself moving outward from a domestic circle of peacemaking to confront violent conflicts in the world. You realize that the reasons for the existence of these destructive situations are much more complex than those for domestic violence. Yet the underlying spirit of peacemaking is applicable to these wider problems. Focus on one area of social destructiveness; let typical scenes from this violence cross your imaginative vision. Surely the added element of structural and institutional injustice looms large in these issues. Because of this difference, other remedies are demanded. Yet the roots of even these problems push into the ground of self- and other-acceptance. If we as Americans felt less threatened by the ideologies and actions of other nations, if we had more confidence about our own best values, we would be less inclined to increase our terrible instruments of violence or to use them.

As you conclude your meditation, imagine again the figure of yourself standing before a world tormented by violence of all kinds. Beside you appears a kindly figure of understanding and dignity who reveals an ideal of the wise elder. You realize that this figure represents in part your own potential for elderhood. This older person invites you to appreciate and embrace peacemaking as the highest priority of your aging journey. With the slow rhythm of your breathing you end the meditation by saying softly as though you were repeating a mantra: "peacemaking elderhood."